Praise for previous editions:

D1222026

"No one wishing to keep a grip on the reality of the world should be without these books." *International Herald Tribune*

Available now:

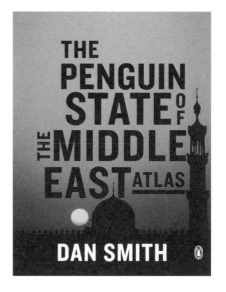

"Invaluable ... I would not be without the complete set on my own shelves." *Times Educational Supplement*

"Fascinating and invaluable." *The Independent*

"A new kind of visual journalism." *New Scientist*

THE

STATE

OF THE

WORLD

ATLAS

TENTH EDITION

DAN SMITH

PENGUIN BOOKS

PENGUIN BOOKS
An imprint of Penguin Random House LLC
penguinrandomhouse.com

This tenth edition first published in Penguin Books 2021

Previous edition published under the title
The Penguin State of the World Atlas: Ninth Edition

Produced for Penguin Books by Myriad Editions,
An imprint of New Internationalist Publications,
The Old Music Hall, 106–108 Cowley Road, Oxford OX4 1JE,
United Kingdom

ISBN 9780143135074 (paperback)

Printed by Jelgavas Tipografija in Latvia

1 3 5 7 9 10 8 6 4 2

Publishing direction: Candida Lacey
Creative direction: Corinne Pearlman
Editing and coordination: Jannet King
Design and graphics: Clare Shepherd
Cartography and original graphics: Isabelle Lewis
Based on an original design by Caroline Beavon

Contents

Introduction

The first step in trying to understand the state of the world is to recognize the simple yet not-so-simple fact that the world is always changing.

Big or small, sudden or slowly building, soon over or with a lasting impact, alterations in the situation and condition of the world and its people are constant.

A lot of that change is progress of one sort or another. Some of what we sometimes call progress is of little worth or merit – useless technological baubles that are modish for a while. And some of it when seen in larger context is downright dangerous – a contribution to global heating or the crisis of air pollution. But in even larger context, human progress is real. More people live longer, healthier lives than ever. Fewer live in extreme poverty than 20 or 30 years ago. The store of human knowledge continues to enlarge. Human rights are respected now in a way that was not dreamed of 200 years ago. And in the first two decades of the 21st century, warfare has taken far fewer human lives than it did in the first two decades of the 20th.

Amid multiple world problems – and perhaps especially writing in 2020 as we wonder what the full effects of the Covid-19 pandemic will be – the point is worth stressing. Human progress has been real over the last century and a half, despite world wars, despite colonialism, despite environmental crises. It has been real and because of that we know that further progress is possible.

It is important to hang onto that because it is also true that a lot of the change we experience is not progress at all. If progress is a journey, it is not about rolling along a smooth path or gliding through space. It is more like lurching in and out of massive potholes in the road or, if you prefer the space metaphor, from one big astral collision to another, juddering all the while under the impact of an unending, randomized shower of meteorites. One thing that matters in trying to understand the state of the world and gauge its progress or regress at any time is to distinguish between the big collisions and the meteorites.

.

The past 30 years – the passage of time normally associated with one human generation – has seen four big moments of change, approximately once a decade. The first came in the years 1989 to 1991, as the Cold War between East and West, between the USSR and its allies on the one side, and the USA and its much richer and larger alliance on the other, came to an end. Not only did the confrontation between the USSR and USA terminate but so also the USSR itself. As the 1990s began, the world order changed, along with the possibilities for what the United Nations could do. Agreements were reached to dismantle tens of thousands of nuclear weapons, military spending started to fall, and the number of countries with a functioning democracy grew throughout the decade. It was not by any means painless. The transition to democracy is often fraught with danger and the first half of the 1990s saw an increase in the number of armed conflicts.

The second big change came in 2001 in the shape of the terrorist attacks of 9/11 in New York and Washington, DC. The peace dividend of the 1990s started to look less peaceful, the long war in Afghanistan that had begun with the Soviet invasion in December 1979 took on a new form as the USA and its allies intervened, and at the same time headed towards war on and then in Iraq.

The third change was the financial crash of 2008 to 2009, which became a general economic crisis in 2009 and 2010. The depth of the crash was different in different countries; economic output recovered but in many of the richer countries in the world, the sense of economic well-being that marked most of the previous two decades has gone for good.

And the fourth big change has come with the Covid-19 pandemic in 2020 – not just the pandemic itself but the economic impact associated with it. At the time of completing this atlas in mid-2020, it is not possible to know what the full impact will be. Though we live in an age that wants instant everything, it remains true that historical significance can only be gauged once the event is well in the past. And even then it is an art rather than a science to understand what it all meant. Nonetheless, the economic impact of the Covid-19 lockdowns – the crash in production, consumption, trade and travel – even though in some aspects recovery may also be equally dramatic, seems likely to be profound and long-lasting.

∎

These events have had a dramatic and lasting impact (or will do in the case of the current pandemic) not simply because of their sheer weight as big events, but also because they interact with other, slower-moving combinations of events. These are the unfolding trends that form the backdrop to the immediate drama. Here we encounter issues such as climate change and today's many-sided environmental crisis. Here is rising inequality in most countries over the past 40-plus years, demographic developments including both population growth – and, more important than the global numbers, where it is concentrated – and urbanization. We see economic growth and seemingly unending technological innovation. And relations between people change, with something closer to gender equality in many countries, with greater acceptance of the rights of LGBTQ+ people, with assumptions about freedoms and responsibilities altering, and with contestation about the rights of different races and ethnic and religious groups within a country.

This atlas offers snapshots of all this. Not one snapshot of the state of the world but, rather, a series of snapshots of diverse aspects of the state of the world as it changes. It captures the big moments and the background trends. It does not and cannot – and does not want to try to – say everything about every, or indeed any, topic. The information here is not the whole story. The treatment of the issue is as an introduction, pointing out a door that, if opened, could be the way towards getting fuller knowledge.

▪

In 2015, the United Nations agreed a potentially era-defining programme – Agenda 2030, with its 17 Sustainable Development Goals (SDGs). If achieved, they could mark the next phase in human progress. Thinking about this agenda in terms of the journey of human progress, I see it as the process of navigating a safe route, increasing the ability to avoid the big collisions, and staying on course despite all the impediments. Under the headline goals there are 169 targets to achieve by 2030. This is human progress as it

The Sustainable Development Goals of the United Nations Agenda 2030

1. End poverty in all its forms everywhere
2. End hunger, achieve food security and improved nutrition and promote sustainable agriculture
3. Ensure healthy lives and promote well-being for all
4. Ensure inclusive and equitable quality education and promote lifelong learning opportunities for all
5. Achieve gender equality and empower all women and girls
6. Ensure availability and sustainable management of water and sanitation for all
7. Ensure access to affordable, reliable, sustainable and modern energy for all
8. Promote sustained, inclusive and sustainable economic growth, full and productive employment and decent work for all
9. Build resilient infrastructure, promote inclusive and sustainable industrialization and foster innovation
10. Reduce inequality within and among countries
11. Make cities and human settlements inclusive, safe, resilient and sustainable
12. Ensure sustainable consumption and production patterns
13. Take urgent action to combat climate change and its impacts
14. Conserve and sustainably use the oceans, seas and marine resources for sustainable development
15. Protect, restore and promote sustainable use of terrestrial ecosystems, sustainably manage forests, combat desertification, and halt and reverse land degradation and halt biodiversity loss
16. Promote peaceful and inclusive societies for sustainable development, provide access to justice for all and build effective, accountable and inclusive institutions at all levels
17. Strengthen the means of implementation and revitalize the Global Partnership for Sustainable Development

could be, towards a better world that is not just imaginable but practicable. In this atlas, I group the issues covered by the SDGs under the heading of five big challenges that face humanity, challenges we must rise to if we are to thrive.

Having looked at who we are – some of the basics of demography, diversity, and dwelling place – the five challenges that confront humanity form the substance of this atlas. They are the production and distribution of wealth and poverty; human rights and the respect with which ordinary people are treated by those in power; the question of war and peace; the health of the people; and the health of the planet.

These are distinct but linked challenges. The effects of the Covid-19 pandemic are not the same for all. Not surprisingly, wealth, privilege and power offer more effective protection to some than is available to all. The same is true of the effects of climate change and many other aspects of environmental deterioration. Throughout the industrial age, rich factory owners managed to live well away from the part of the city their factories polluted. There is no health or environmental issue that is purely about physiological health or how things are in nature. The source of the problem, how it is defined, the allocation of resources to address it are all shaped by how society is governed. Social inequalities and lack of respect for human rights often mean there is no way to express grievances except through anger, to which power responds through repression. That explosive mixture can quickly generate political instability and open armed conflict. The socially destabilising effects of climate change and environmental crisis only add to those pressures.

Cooperation is the new realism

Recent years have seen a distinct decline in how well these challenges are addressed. This is the tenth edition of this atlas. For the ninth in 2013, summing it up, I had a relatively positive assessment on rights and respect, partly because democracy was growing, as well as on war and peace, and on health. But any progress on wealth and poverty was marred by growing inequalities and damage to the natural environment. So on three of the five challenges, the record, while not perfect, was not bad; on the other two, the record was clearly deficient. Since then, while the statistics of democracy remain good, its quality is weaker in many countries. Worse, geopolitics have turned toxic, the number of armed conflicts has increased, and the scale of military preparations now is back to Cold War levels. And on the health front, there is the pandemic.

So there is more bad news than a few years ago. But the tools for improvement are available. The UN's Agenda 2030 and the SDGs themselves demonstrate that. We can see it in the snapshots in this atlas when we look at peace operations, at advances in healthcare, at the possibilities for reshaping economic functioning so the natural environment is better respected. Further, in some places, the tools are in use. We can see them in initiatives to build peace and support neighbours in highly diverse local communities; in small-scale environmental protection projects and some initiatives that are pretty large scale; in choices some people are making to live lives and to run businesses in ways that are more in tune with the rhythms of nature.

One characteristic of world politics today is a visibly declining appetite for international cooperation among the biggest players and many of the smaller ones. That is the severest single difficulty to overcome so the work of improvement and progress can resume in good order. None of the challenges and problems depicted in this atlas can be successfully addressed by any state acting alone. Not even the biggest, the richest, or the most populous. Going it alone is a fantasy; cooperation is the new realism.

If we face the bad news, perhaps we will see that it is not so bad. There are so many other things happening. And that should be a spur to action, to take the decisions that are needed to stem the rise of inequality, ensure our rights are respected, expand the world's zone of peace again, keep improving public health and prepare better against the next pandemic, and put our relationship with nature onto a healthier footing. And above all, to start working together to those ends.

·

Finally, my thanks to those who make this book possible but don't get on the title page. In the Myriad team, Jannet King has once again been the editor for this tenth edition in the series, assiduous and sharp yet kindly. The cartography and visuals are the work of Clare Shepherd and of Isabelle Lewis, within the design framework established by Corinne Pearlman. All this happens under the inspiring and supportive leadership of Candida Lacey. The research assistance, which means all the hard work, was done by Jakob Faller.

It was a semi-surreal experience to complete the work on this edition in the midst of the first wave of the Covid-19 pandemic, even if doing it in the lockdown-lite of Sweden rather than the full-on isolation of many other countries. What helped keep me sane in that was family – Åsa, Felix and Bob close at hand, and further away in two homes in one city, Jake, Jess, Josie and Jed, and Rebecca, Marcus and Zac. My thanks and love to you all whether you knew how much you were helping or not.

Dan Smith
Stockholm
June 2020

Who we are

What is the name of our age? It continues to be the age of more, most, and never before.

There are more people, living in more countries, and more of us living in cities, than at any time. And along with that come things never before experienced, so much so that the idea of "the new normal" has become the defining cliché of our time.

New – the consequences of climate change.

New – the loss of biodiversity and of land quality.

New – the acidification of the oceans.

New – the crisis of air pollution.

New – plastic garbage covering the ocean.

New – our dependence on cyberspace, and with it vulnerability to its failure.

New – the cycle of pandemics from SARS to MERS to Covid-19.

New – the combination of all of the above.

It is only just over 200 years ago – less than a blink of an eye in the timescale of the planet, and not much more in the timescale of human beings – that the world's population passed the 1 billion mark. Today, there are just under 8 billion of us. Despite signs of deceleration in the rate of growth, world population is still projected to increase by another 2 billion people to around 10 billion by 2050. By then, towns and cities are expected to hold just over two-thirds of humanity.

There has never been demographic change on such a huge scale. The movement from the countryside to the cities in the industrial revolution two centuries ago has nothing on this. Nor has migration from Europe to the American New World between the mid-19th century and the early 20th century – just 30 million people. Compared to that, the increase in the global population so far this century is almost 100 million every year, and urban population growth is even faster.

Because there are more of us, we inevitably consume more of everything. But technological advance means that we also consume massively more per person. Our population, eight times that of 200 years ago, produces over 50 times the economic output, and uses more than 60 times as much water and 75 times as much energy.

The figures testify to the creativity unleashed through the Industrial Revolution. They should also encourage us to ask: For how long can we continue?

States of the world

SVALBARD (Nor.)

GREENLAND (Den)

FAROE IS. (Den)

ICELAND

CANADA

FINLAND

NORWAY
SWEDEN
ES
LAT.
LITH.

UK
IS. OF MAN (UK) DENMARK
IRELAND
NETH.
GERMANY POLAND
CHANNEL IS. (UK) BEL. CZ.REP.
LUX. SLOVAKIA
FRANCE SW AUS. HUN.
SL
ITALY CR. B-H K
MONT. S.
N. MAC.
ALB.

ST PIERRE & MIQUELON (Fr)

USA

PORTUGAL
SPAIN

GIBRALTAR (UK)

TUNISIA
MALTA

GREECE

BERMUDA (UK)

MOROCCO

MEXICO

BAHAMAS
TURKS & CAICOS IS. (UK)
PUERTO RICO
DOMINICAN
REP.
HAITI
CUBA

CAYMAN IS. (UK)
JAMAICA HAITI

BELIZE
GUATEMALA HONDURAS
EL SALVADOR
NICARAGUA
COSTA RICA

PANAMA

ANGUILLA (UK)
VIRGIN IS.
(UK) ST MARTIN (Fr)
SINT MAARTEN (Neths)
ST BARTHÉLEMY (Fr)
VIRGIN IS. (USA) ANTIGUA & BARBUDA
ST KITTS & NEVIS GUADELOUPE (Fr)
MONTSERRAT (UK) DOMINICA
MARTINIQUE (Fr)
ARUBA (Neths) GRENADA ST LUCIA
BARBADOS
CURAÇAO (Neths) ST VINCENT & GRENADINES
BONAIRE (Neths) TRINIDAD & TOBAGO

WESTERN
SAHARA (Mor.)

ALGERIA

LIBYA

CAPE
VERDE
SENEGAL
GAMBIA
GUINEA-BISSAU

MAURITANIA

MALI

NIGER

CHAD

GUINEA
SIERRA LEONE CÔTE
LIBERIA D'IVOIRE

BURKINA
FASO
GHANA BENIN
TOGO

NIGERIA

C.A.R.

CAMEROON

VENEZUELA GUYANA
COLOMBIA SURINAME
FRENCH GUIANA (Fr)

ECUADOR

PERU

BRAZIL

EQUATORIAL
GUINEA
SÃO TOME
& PRINCIPE GABON

CONGO

ANGOLA

ST HELENA, ASCENSION & TRISTAN
(UK)

NAMIBIA

BOLIVIA

PARAGUAY

CHILE ARGENTINA

URUGUAY

FALKLANDS IS. (UK)

S GEORGIA & S SANDWICH IS. (UK)

Sovereignty

Effective independence gained
by existing states

before 11 November 1918

11 November 1918 –
23 October 1945

24 October 1945 –
8 November 1989

9 November 1989 –
30 September 2019

not a sovereign
state (affiliation)

RUSSIA

BELARUS

UKRAINE

MOLDOVA

ROM

BUL

GEORGIA

ARMENIA AZER.

TURKEY

CYPRUS (TURK)

CYPRUS LEB.

ISRAEL

SYRIA

PAL. AUTHORITY

JORDAN

IRAQ

KUWAIT

BAHRAIN

QATAR

U.A.E.

EGYPT

SAUDI
ARABIA

OMAN

SUDAN

ERITREA

YEMEN

DJIBOUTI

Somaliland

SOUTH
SUDAN

ETHIOPIA

Puntland

D.R.
CONGO

UGANDA

KENYA

RWANDA

BURUNDI

TANZANIA

SEYCHELLES

COMOROS

MAYOTTE (Fr)

ZAMBIA

MALAWI

MADAGASCAR

MAURITIUS

ZIMBABWE

BOTSWANA

MOZAMBIQUE

RÉUNION (Fr)

SOUTH
AFRICA

SWAZILAND

LESOTHO

KAZAKHSTAN

UZBEKISTAN

KYRGYZSTAN

TURKMEN.

TAJIKISTAN

IRAN

AFGHANISTAN

PAKISTAN

NEPAL

BHUTAN

INDIA

BANGLADESH

MYANMAR

LAOS

THAILAND

VIETNAM

CAMBODIA

SRI LANKA

MALDIVES

MONGOLIA

CHINA

MACAO SAR (CHINA)

HONG KONG (SAR CHINA)

NORTH
KOREA

SOUTH
KOREA

JAPAN

TAIWAN

PHILIPPINES

BRUNEI

MALAYSIA

SINGAPORE

INDONESIA

CHRISTMAS IS. (Aus)

TIMOR-LESTE

PAPUA
NEW
GUINEA

SOLOMON
ISLANDS

AUSTRALIA

NEW
ZEALAND

GUAM (USA)

NORTHERN MARIANA IS. (USA)

MICRONESIA, FED. ST. OF

MARSHALL ISLANDS

PALAU

NAURU

KIRIBATI

TUVALU

TOKELAU

AMERICAN SAMOA (USA)

SAMOA

WALLIS & FUTUNA IS. (Fr)

VANUATU

FIJI

COOK IS. (NZ)

NIUE (NZ)

TONGA

NEW CALEDONIA (Fr)

NORFOLK IS. (Aus)

FRENCH POLYNESIA (Fr)

PITCAIRN IS. (UK)

State formation

Number of states gaining effective independence
in each decade including states that no longer exist

as of September 2019

▬▬▬ before 11 November 1918

▬▬▬ 11 November 1918 – 23 October 1945

▬▬▬ 24 October 1945 – 8 November 1989

▬▬▬ 9 November 1989 – 30 September 2019

Some of our sense of who we are comes from where we were born and grew up – our countries, most of which are quite recent creations. In 1945, the United Nations was founded by just 51 states, some of which were not fully independent at the time (and the defeated states in World War II were initially excluded). Today, the UN has 193 member states.

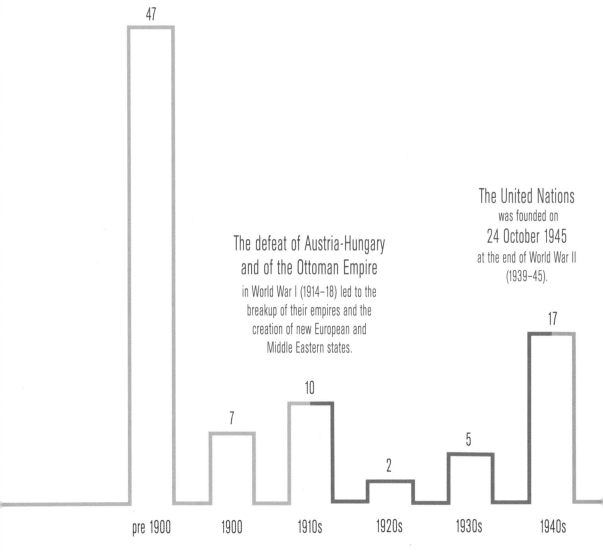

47

The defeat of Austria-Hungary and of the Ottoman Empire

in World War I (1914–18) led to the breakup of their empires and the creation of new European and Middle Eastern states.

The United Nations
was founded on
24 October 1945
at the end of World War II
(1939–45).

17

10

7

5

2

pre 1900   1900   1910s   1920s   1930s   1940s

Over the past century, states have won, lost, and regained independence, divided and (re-)unified, often but not always against a background of war and bloodshed.

Some have become formally independent before achieving real independence; with others, it has been the other way round.

On other pages, this atlas shows many ways – economic, environmental, political – in which independent states do not have full sovereignty in the modern world – yet the evidence is clear that sovereignty is a highly desirable political commodity. The age of forming new states is not yet over.

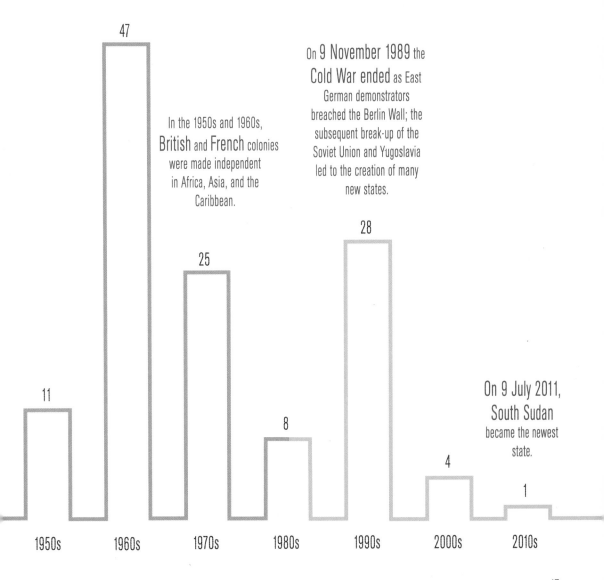

47

In the 1950s and 1960s, **British** and **French** colonies were made independent in Africa, Asia, and the Caribbean.

On **9 November 1989** the **Cold War ended** as East German demonstrators breached the Berlin Wall; the subsequent break-up of the Soviet Union and Yugoslavia led to the creation of many new states.

28

25

11

8

On **9 July 2011**, **South Sudan** became the newest state.

4

1

| 1950s | 1960s | 1970s | 1980s | 1990s | 2000s | 2010s |

Population

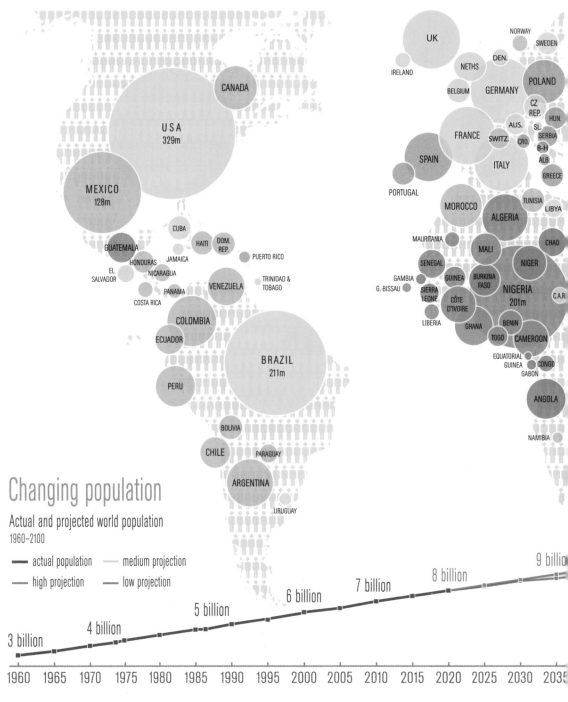

CANADA

USA
329m

MEXICO
128m

CUBA

GUATEMALA
HONDURAS
EL SALVADOR
NICARAGUA
COSTA RICA
PANAMA

HAITI
DOM. REP.
JAMAICA

PUERTO RICO

TRINIDAD & TOBAGO

VENEZUELA

COLOMBIA

ECUADOR

PERU

BRAZIL
211m

BOLIVIA

CHILE
PARAGUAY

ARGENTINA
URUGUAY

UK

NORWAY
SWEDEN

IRELAND

NETHS
DEN.

BELGIUM
GERMANY
POLAND

CZ REP.
HUN.

FRANCE
AUS.
SL
SERBIA
SWITZ.
CRO.
B-H
ALB.

SPAIN
ITALY

GREECE

PORTUGAL

MOROCCO
TUNISIA
LIBYA

ALGERIA

MAURITANIA
MALI
CHAD

SENEGAL
NIGER

GAMBIA
GUINEA
BURKINA FASO
NIGERIA
201m
C.A.R

G.-BISSAU
SIERRA LEONE
CÔTE D'IVOIRE

LIBERIA
GHANA
BENIN

TOGO
CAMEROON

EQUATORIAL GUINEA
CONGO
GABON

ANGOLA

NAMIBIA

Changing population

Actual and projected world population
1960–2100

—— actual population   —— medium projection
—— high projection   —— low projection

3 billion

4 billion

5 billion

6 billion

7 billion

8 billion

9 billio

1960 1965 1970 1975 1980 1985 1990 1995 2000 2005 2010 2015 2020 2025 2030 2035

People in the world
Annual percentage change
2019

 3.0% or more
2.0% – 2.9%

 1.0% – 1.9%
0.0% – 0.9%

 -0.1% – -2.8%
◯ 1 million people

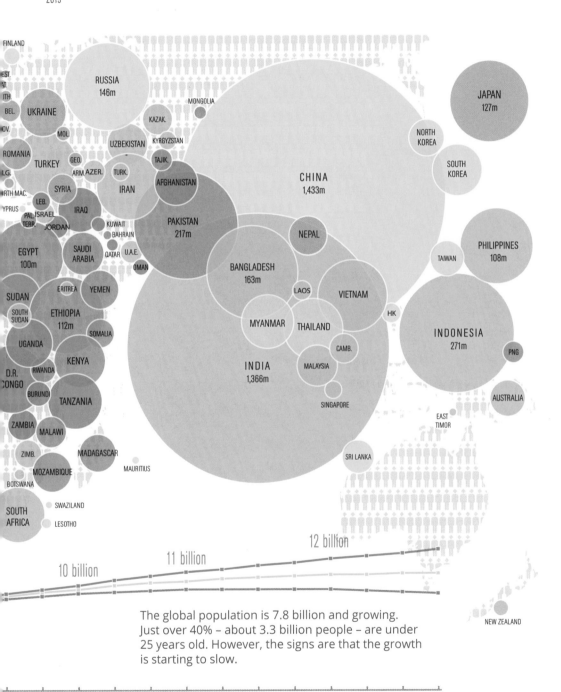

FINLAND

EST.
LAT.
LITH.
BEL.
MOV.

RUSSIA
146m

MONGOLIA

UKRAINE

KAZAK.

ROMANIA
TURKEY
LG.

MOL

UZBEKISTAN
KYRGYZSTAN

GEO.
ARM. AZER.
TURK.

TAJIK.

JAPAN
127m

NORTH
KOREA

NORTH MAC.
CYPRUS

SYRIA
LEB.
PAL. ISRAEL
TERR.
JORDAN

IRAN

IRAQ

AFGHANISTAN

KUWAIT
BAHRAIN

CHINA
1,433m

SOUTH
KOREA

EGYPT
100m

SAUDI
ARABIA

QATAR U.A.E.

OMAN

PAKISTAN
217m

NEPAL

BANGLADESH
163m

TAIWAN

PHILIPPINES
108m

SUDAN

SOUTH
SUDAN

ERITREA

ETHIOPIA
112m

YEMEN

SOMALIA

LAOS

VIETNAM

HK

UGANDA

MYANMAR

THAILAND

INDONESIA
271m

PNG

D.R.
CONGO

RWANDA

BURUNDI

KENYA

CAMB.

INDIA
1,366m

MALAYSIA

TANZANIA

SINGAPORE

AUSTRALIA

ZAMBIA
MALAWI

EAST
TIMOR

ZIMB.

MADAGASCAR

MAURITIUS

MOZAMBIQUE

BOTSWANA

SRI LANKA

SOUTH
AFRICA

SWAZILAND

LESOTHO

12 billion

11 billion

10 billion

NEW ZEALAND

The global population is 7.8 billion and growing.
Just over 40% – about 3.3 billion people – are under
25 years old. However, the signs are that the growth
is starting to slow.

2040 2045 2050 2055 2060 2065 2070 2075 2080 2085 2090 2095 2100

Life expectancy

Living longer

Average years life expectancy at birth

1870–2016

29.7 · 32 · 34.1 · 48 · 60 · 65.2 · 66.5 · 70.1 · 72

Life expectancy at birth

2016

Legend:
- 53 – 59 years
- 60 – 69 years
- 70 – 79 years
- 80 – 84 years

Changes in life expectancy

↑ increase of ten years or more
↓ decrease of ten years or more

Average life expectancy has never been higher. It continues to grow as general levels of health and public sanitation continue to improve. In this respect, the Covid-19 pandemic will have almost no statistical effect.

In southern Africa during the 2000s, the proportion of the population infected by HIV/AIDS was up to 30 times the world average. This combined with other diseases to reduce average life expectancy in the region, but drug treatments for HIV/AIDS and public health campaigns have had a noticeable positive impact in recent years.

Women and men

Women in the world

Female population as
percentage of
total population
2018

- less than 40%
- 40% – 48%
- 49% – 51%
- 52% – 54%

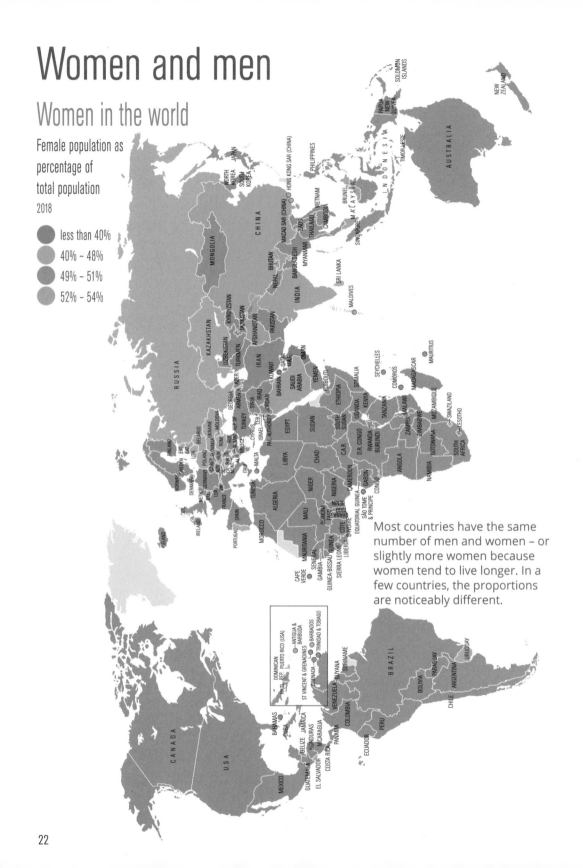

Most countries have the same
number of men and women – or
slightly more women because
women tend to live longer. In a
few countries, the proportions
are noticeably different.

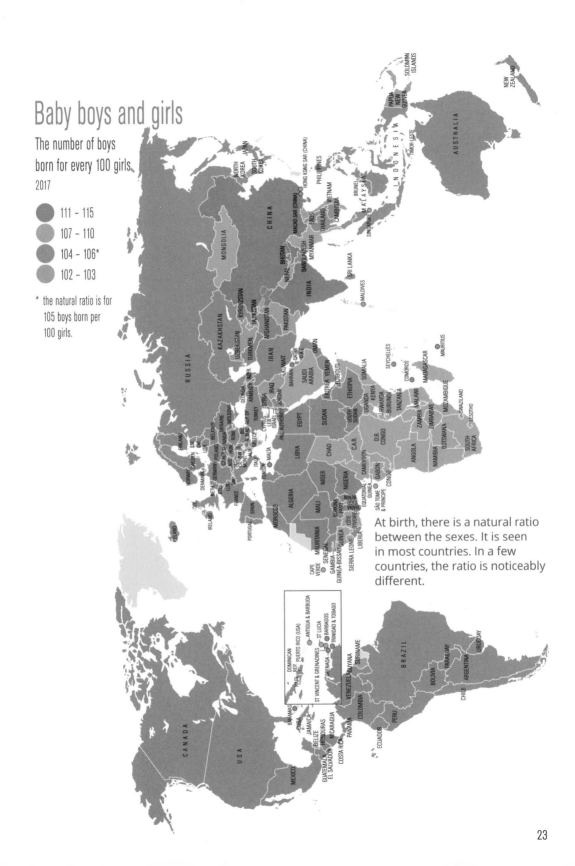

Baby boys and girls

The number of boys
born for every 100 girls

2017

- 111 – 115
- 107 – 110
- 104 – 106*
- 102 – 103

* the natural ratio is for
105 boys born per
100 girls.

At birth, there is a natural ratio
between the sexes. It is seen
in most countries. In a few
countries, the ratio is noticeably
different.

Ethnicity and diversity

Minorities and indigenous peoples

As a percentage of the population*

2019 or latest available data
* definitions differ among countries

- less than 10%
- 10% – 29%
- 30% – 49%
- 50% or more (there is no majority group)
- data lacking or inadequate

Part of human diversity lies in our membership of large groups – nations, ethnic groups, races, tribes, clans. How these are defined varies from one culture to another. How important they are varies both from one person to the next and from time to time. Groups take on the most explicit importance for their members when they are or feel threatened – whether by day-to-day discrimination and ill treatment or by traumatic events as in war.

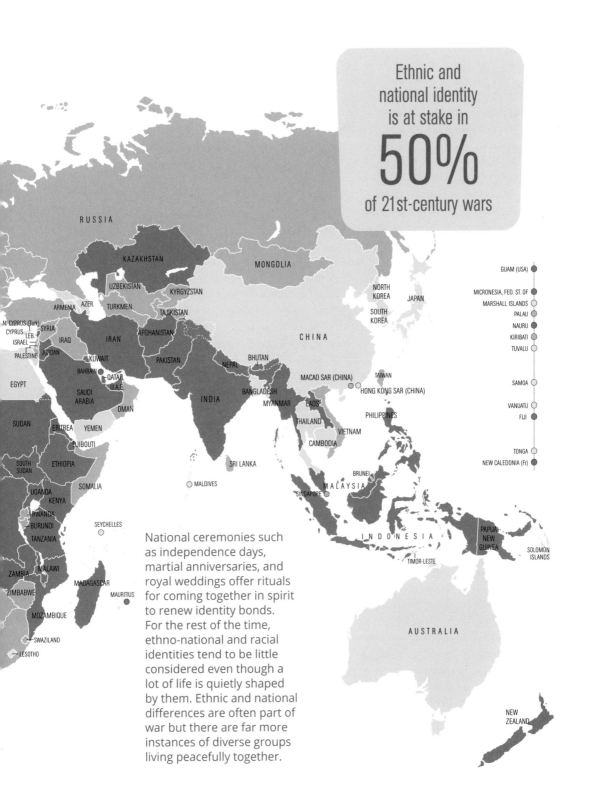

RUSSIA

KAZAKHSTAN

MONGOLIA

UZBEKISTAN
KYRGYZSTAN

NORTH
KOREA   JAPAN

ARMENIA   AZER.   TURKMEN.   TAJIKISTAN

SOUTH
KOREA

N. CYPRUS (Turk)
CYPRUS   LEB.   SYRIA
ISRAEL
PALESTINE   IRAQ   JORDAN   IRAN   AFGHANISTAN

CHINA

KUWAIT   PAKISTAN   NEPAL   BHUTAN

BAHRAIN   QATAR
U.A.E.

EGYPT

SAUDI
ARABIA   OMAN

INDIA   BANGLADESH   MYANMAR

MACAO SAR (CHINA)   TAIWAN
HONG KONG SAR (CHINA)

LAOS

SUDAN   ERITREA   YEMEN

THAILAND   PHILIPPINES

VIETNAM

DJIBOUTI

CAMBODIA

SOUTH
SUDAN   ETHIOPIA

SRI LANKA

BRUNEI

UGANDA
KENYA   SOMALIA

MALDIVES

MALAYSIA

SINGAPORE

RWANDA
BURUNDI
TANZANIA   SEYCHELLES

INDONESIA

PAPUA
NEW
GUINEA

SOLOMON
ISLANDS

ZAMBIA   MALAWI

TIMOR-LESTE

ZIMBABWE   MADAGASCAR

MAURITIUS

MOZAMBIQUE

AUSTRALIA

SWAZILAND

LESOTHO

GUAM (USA)

MICRONESIA, FED. ST. OF

MARSHALL ISLANDS

PALAU

NAURU

KIRIBATI

TUVALU

SAMOA

VANUATU

FIJI

TONGA

NEW CALEDONIA (Fr)

National ceremonies such
as independence days,
martial anniversaries, and
royal weddings offer rituals
for coming together in spirit
to renew identity bonds.
For the rest of the time,
ethno-national and racial
identities tend to be little
considered even though a
lot of life is quietly shaped
by them. Ethnic and national
differences are often part of
war but there are far more
instances of diverse groups
living peacefully together.

NEW
ZEALAND

Migrants

People living in country other than that in which they were born as a percentage of total population
2017

- 50% or more
- 30% – 49%
- 10% – 29%
- less than 10%

Worldwide, some
258 million
people live outside their country of birth

Including refugees and migrant workers, just 3.3% of the world's population are international migrants. Migration within countries is three times greater.

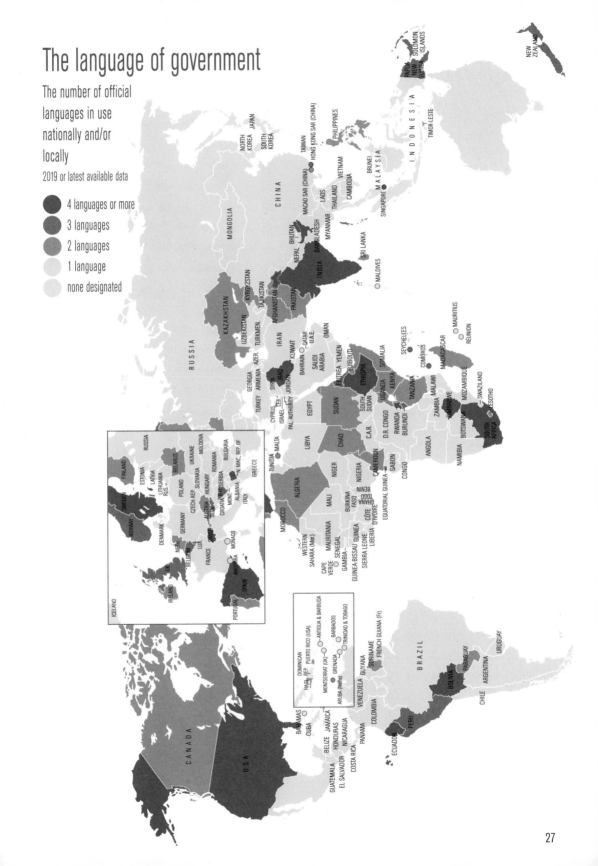

The language of government

The number of official
languages in use
nationally and/or
locally

2019 or latest available data

- 4 languages or more
- 3 languages
- 2 languages
- 1 language
- none designated

Religious beliefs

The vast majority of people profess a religious faith. Although professing a faith on a population census form and actually practising it are two very different things, faith is, for many, a basic marker of identity. Shared religious conviction can unite people where other things divide them, and even between different faiths there is significant ethical common ground and a shared openness to the spiritual and immaterial.

But religious identity coincides with other markers of identity – regional, national, ethnic, and cultural. When and where religious leaders cannot or will not restrain the way in which adherents to different faiths express their differences, conflicts can overheat and explode. Some of the world's most brutal violence is – and has been throughout history – inflicted in the name of religion. And some of the worst violence is over differences within the same religion: between Protestants and Catholic Christians, or between Sunni and Shi'a Muslims. Yet common to all major religions is the over-riding value of peace.

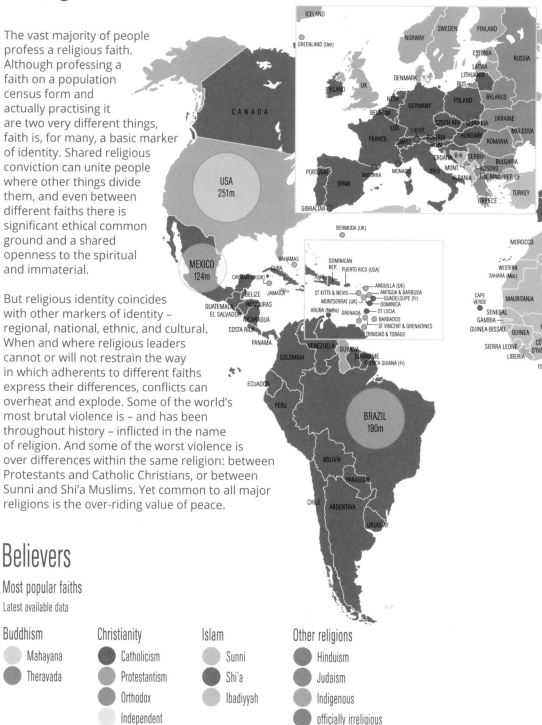

Believers

Most popular faiths

Latest available data

Buddhism
- Mahayana
- Theravada

Christianity
- Catholicism
- Protestantism
- Orthodox
- Independent

Islam
- Sunni
- Shi'a
- Ibadiyyah

Other religions
- Hinduism
- Judaism
- Indigenous
- officially irreligious

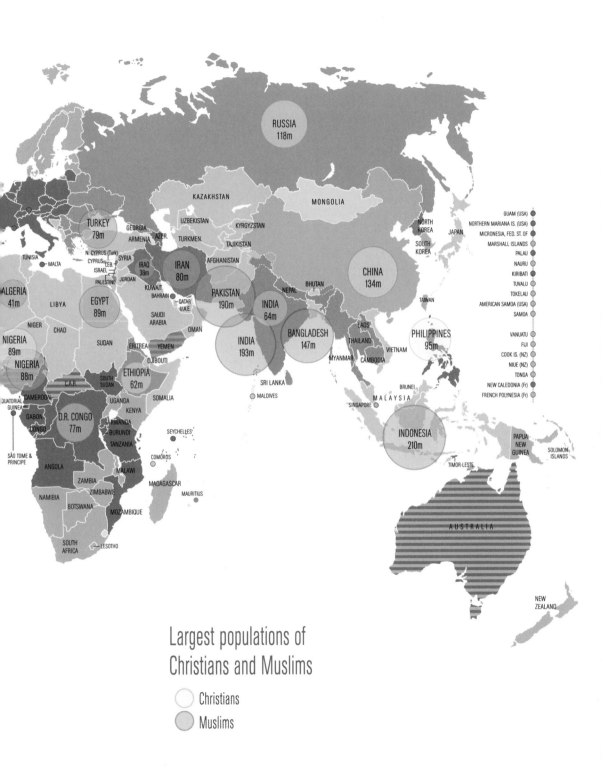

RUSSIA
118m

KAZAKHSTAN

MONGOLIA

NORTH
KOREA

JAPAN

SOUTH
KOREA

TURKEY
79m

GEORGIA

ARMENIA   AZER.

TURKMEN.

UZBEKISTAN

KYRGYZSTAN

TAJIKISTAN

AFGHANISTAN

N. CYPRUS (Turk.)

TUNISIA   • MALTA

CYPRUS   LEB.

ISRAEL   SYRIA

PALESTINE   JORDAN

IRAQ
38m

IRAN
80m

PAKISTAN
190m

NEPAL

BHUTAN

CHINA
134m

TAIWAN

GUAM (USA)

NORTHERN MARIANA IS. (USA)

MICRONESIA, FED. ST. OF

MARSHALL ISLANDS

PALAU

NAURU

KIRIBATI

TUVALU

TOKELAU

AMERICAN SAMOA (USA)

SAMOA

ALGERIA
41m

LIBYA

EGYPT
89m

KUWAIT

BAHRAIN

QATAR

U.A.E.

SAUDI
ARABIA

OMAN

INDIA
64m

NIGER

CHAD

SUDAN

ERITREA   YEMEN

DJIBOUTI

INDIA
193m

SRI LANKA

MALDIVES

BANGLADESH
147m

LAOS

THAILAND

MYANMAR   CAMBODIA

VIETNAM

PHILIPPINES
95m

VANUATU

FIJI

COOK IS. (NZ)

NIUE (NZ)

TONGA

NEW CALEDONIA (Fr)

FRENCH POLYNESIA (Fr)

NIGERIA
89m

NIGERIA
88m

ETHIOPIA
62m

C.A.R.

SOUTH
SUDAN

SOMALIA

EQUATORIAL
GUINEA

CAMEROON

UGANDA

KENYA

BRUNEI

MALAYSIA

SINGAPORE

GABON

CONGO

D.R. CONGO
77m

RWANDA

BURUNDI

TANZANIA

SEYCHELLES

INDONESIA
210m

PAPUA
NEW
GUINEA

SOLOMON
ISLANDS

SÃO TOMÉ &
PRINCIPE

ANGOLA

ZAMBIA

MALAWI

COMOROS

MADAGASCAR

MAURITIUS

TIMOR-LESTE

NAMIBIA

ZIMBABWE

BOTSWANA

MOZAMBIQUE

SOUTH
AFRICA

LESOTHO

AUSTRALIA

NEW
ZEALAND

Largest populations of
Christians and Muslims

◯ Christians

◯ Muslims

World faiths

Estimated number of followers

Latest available data

Christianity
- Catholicism
- Protestantism
- Orthodox
- other

Islam
- Sunni
- Shi'a

Other religions
- Buddhism
- Hinduism
- Judaism
- Sikhism
- other religions

👤 2.5 million people

4,368 million

Islam is the world's fastest growing religion. On current trends, by 2060 there may be as many Muslims as Christians.

1,716 million

1,029 million

831 million

530 million

26 million

15 million

Non-believers

People who profess no religion
as a percentage of population

Latest available data

- **20% or more**
- **10% – 19%**
- **fewer than 10%**

Literacy and education

1 in 7 adults is functionally illiterate

Haiti

Mauritania   Mali
Senegal   Niger
         Gambia Burkina   Chad
Guinea-Bissau   Faso   Nigeria
         Guinea
Sierra Leone   Togo
         Liberia Côte Benin
              d'Ivoire

Literacy is simultaneously a functional need for modern societies, a basic tool for individual advancement, and a personal source of knowledge, access to the world, and satisfaction. Thanks to a major international effort, trends this century have been positive, although there remain places where more than half of adults are functionally illiterate, which means they are unable to read or write a short statement about their everyday life.

Adult illiteracy

- ● 70% or more
- ● 50% – 69%
- ● 35% – 49%

Afghanistan
Pakistan Nepal
Bhutan
Iraq
Yemen
Sudan
Eritrea
South
Sudan Ethiopia
C.A.R
Burundi
Comoros
Malawi
Mozambique
Papua New
Guinea
Timor-Leste

66%
of illiterate
adults
are women

Primary education

Percentage of children
of the correct age
enrolled in primary school

2017 or latest available data

- 90% or more
- 70% – 89%
- 50% – 69%
- 30% – 49%
- no data

Where the foundations have
been laid, primary education
has shown real forward
movement, although in Africa
and some other areas, progress
in secondary and tertiary
education remains slow.

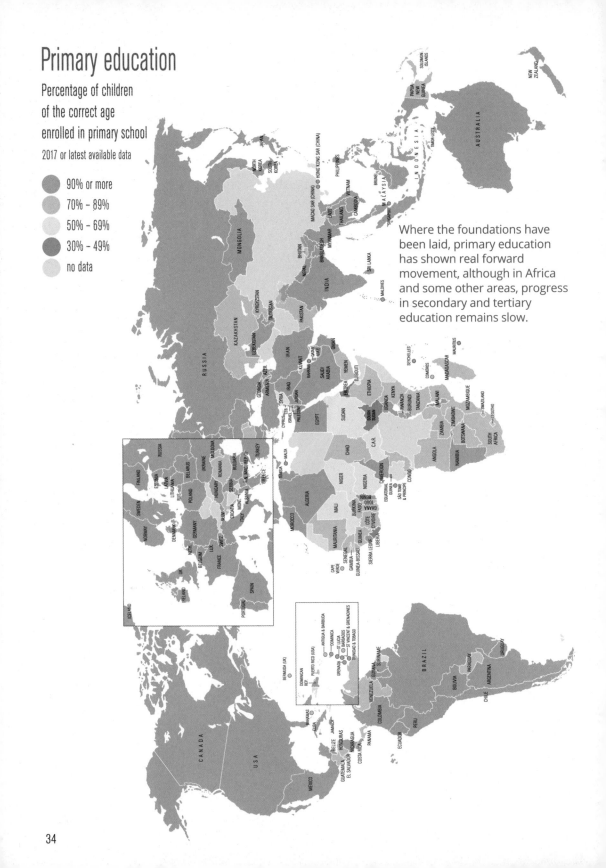

Secondary education

Percentage of children of the correct age enrolled in secondary school

2017 or latest available data

- ● 90% or more
- ● 70% – 89%
- ○ 50% – 69%
- ● 30% – 49%
- ● fewer than 30%

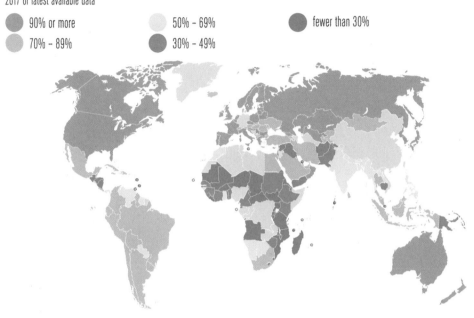

Tertiary education

Percentage of people of the correct age enrolled in tertiary education

2017 or latest available data

- ● 90% or more
- ● 70% – 89%
- ○ 50% – 69%
- ● 30% – 49%
- ● fewer than 30%

Urbanization

CANADA

USA

MEXICO

BAHAMAS

CUBA

BELIZE
GUATEMALA
EL SALVADOR
HONDURAS
NICARAGUA
COSTA RICA
PANAMA

JAMAICA
HAITI
DOMINICAN REP.
PUERTO RICO
ANTIGUA & BARBUDA
ST KITTS & NEVIS
DOMINICA
GRENADA
ST LUCIA
BARBADOS
ST VINCENT & GRENADINES
TRINIDAD & TOBAGO

VENEZUELA
GUYANA
SURINAME
COLOMBIA

ECUADOR

PERU

BRAZIL

BOLIVIA

PARAGUAY

CHILE

URUGUAY
ARGENTINA

ICELAND
NORWAY
FINLAND
SWEDEN
ESTONIA
LATVIA
DENMARK
LITHUANIA
IRELAND
UK
NETH.
BEL.
GERMANY
POLAND
BELARUS
LUX.
CZ. REP.
SL.
FRANCE
AUS.
SL.
HUN.
ROM.
SWITZ.
CROATIA
B-H
SERB.
BUL.
M.—
ITALY
ALB.
N. MAC.
PORTUGAL
SPAIN
GREECE
TUNISIA

MOROCCO

MAL

ALGERIA

LIBYA

CAPE VERDE
MAURITANIA
MALI
NIGER
CHA
SENEGAL
GAMBIA
BURKINA FASO
NIGERIA
GUINEA-BISSAU GUINEA
CÔTE D'IVOIRE
GHANA
TOGO
BENIN
SIERRA LEONE
LIBERIA
CAMEROON
C.A
EQUATORIAL GUINEA
SAO TOME & PRINCIPE
GABON
CONGO
ANGO

NAMIBIA

SOUT
AFRIC

Urban population

As a percentage of total population
2017

- 90% or more
- 70% – 89%
- 50% – 69%
- 30% – 49%
- 10% – 29%
- no data
- metropolitan areas with 10 million or more inhabitants

RUSSIA

UKRAINE
MOLDOVA
GEORGIA
TURKEY ARMENIA AZER.
CYPRUS SYRIA
LEB.
ISRAEL JORDAN
PAL.
IRAQ
KUWAIT
BAHRAIN
QATAR
UAE
EGYPT
SAUDI ARABIA
OMAN

KAZAKHSTAN

MONGOLIA

UZBEKISTAN KYRGYZSTAN
TURKMEN. TAJIKISTAN
AFGHANISTAN
IRAN
PAKISTAN
NEPAL BHUTAN
INDIA
BANGLADESH
MYANMAR

CHINA

NORTH KOREA
SOUTH KOREA
JAPAN

Hong Kong SAR
Macau SAR
LAOS
THAILAND VIETNAM
CAMBODIA
PHILIPPINES

SUDAN
ERITREA YEMEN
DJIBOUTI
SOUTH SUDAN
ETHIOPIA
SOMALIA
UGANDA
KENYA
DEM. EP. OF ONGO
RWANDA
BURUNDI
TANZANIA
COMOROS
ZAMBIA MALAWI
ZIMBABWE
BOTSWANA
MOZAMBIQUE
SWAZILAND
LESOTHO
MADAGASCAR
MAURITIUS
SEYCHELLES

MALDIVES
SRI LANKA

BRUNEI
MALAYSIA
SINGAPORE

INDONESIA
EAST TIMOR

PAPUA NEW GUINEA
SOLOMON ISLANDS

AUSTRALIA

NEW ZEALAND

- MICRONESIA, FED. STATES OF
- PALAU
- NAURU
- KIRIBATI
- TUVALU
- SAMOA
- VANUATU
- FIJI
- TONGA

37

Urban dwellers

More than half of the world's people live in towns and cities and the number keeps growing. Back in 1800, some 3% lived in cities. In 2020, the corresponding figure is about 55%. And one projection is that by 2050 it will be 6.8 billion.

In 1950, the world's ten largest cities were in Europe and the Americas. But most major cities in Europe are now static in size, or declining, as improved transport and communications reduce the economic benefits of people living in highly concentrated urban environments.

The urbanization of recent years has happened largely in the poor, middle-income and developing countries, where people still move from the countryside to the cities in search of jobs and livelihoods.

Asia is leading the field in terms of megacities, but although it is these giant urban conglomerations that vie with each other to be the largest financial centre, or location of the world's tallest building, only one in eight of all urban residents actually lives in such cities. The majority of urban dwellers reside in small towns and cities of a more modest size and character.

Ten largest cities

In 1950
1 million people

In 2018
1 million people

Global urban population:
1950: 751 million
2020: 4,379 million

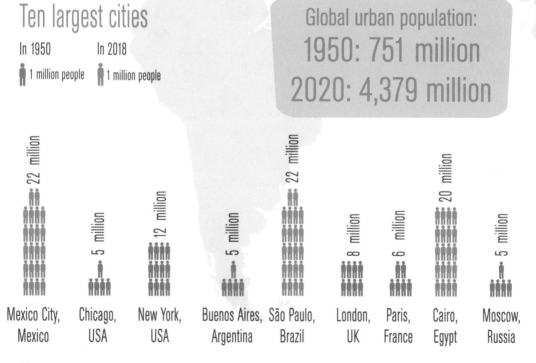

Mexico City, Mexico	Chicago, USA	New York, USA	Buenos Aires, Argentina	São Paulo, Brazil	London, UK	Paris, France	Cairo, Egypt	Moscow, Russia
22 million	5 million	12 million	5 million	22 million	8 million	6 million	20 million	5 million

City scale

Number of people living in different sizes of urban conglomeration
2018

 529 million people living in megacities of 10 million or more

1.25 billion people living in major cities of 1–10 million

2.4 billion people living in towns and cities of fewer than 1 million

 20 million
Mumbai, India

29 million
Delhi, India

5 million
Kolkata, India

 20 million
Dhaka, Bangladesh

20 million
Beijing, China

 4 million | 26 million
Shanghai, China

 7 million | 19 million
Osaka, Japan

 11 million | 37 million
Tokyo, Japan

Wealth and poverty

The 21st century opened with almost a decade of impressive economic growth worldwide during which global output nearly doubled. Since then, there have been two massive economic crises – 2008 to 2009, and 2020.

The crisis of 2008 to 2009 was financial – debt was too high and the collateral was inadequate. Finally, the party ended. Economic slowdown and recession were widespread. Public spending on health, education, and welfare was cut in many countries. Some countries remained in the grip of austerity a decade later but others had fared better and recovered during the 2010s.

Then, at the start of 2020, came Covid-19, a pandemic seemingly originating in the transfer of a virus from animal to human. Countries locked down. Many governments closed most workplaces along with schools and universities; they prevented most travel into, out of, and even within the country; almost all people stayed at home, coming out only for essential shopping; in many cases children were not allowed out of the home at all.

The full scale of the economic impact of Covid-19 will not be clear for some time. The short-term effects were a true economic shock. China's economy, which had grown steadily for almost 50 years, shrank in the first three months of 2020. In the USA 33 million people filed for unemployment benefit in March and April. Never, in modern times, had so many jobs disappeared so fast. Some governments footed part of the bill for workers' wages but could not keep that going long-term. Global airline travel collapsed by 99 per cent. Authoritative projections indicated world trade could slump by as much as one-third.

Evidence soon started to build that the effects of Covid-19 are not socially equal. The poor are hardest hit because they almost certainly lack savings, living hand to mouth, with no health insurance – or in some cases, with health insurance attached to their jobs, which they had lost. Statistics have revealed a general increase in inequality in the richer countries since the 1970s, and the effects of Covid-19 will be sharper in many places as a result. Without sustained counter-measures by governments, inequalities are likely to worsen. Extreme poverty has fallen sharply over the past three decades but there were signs in the first half of 2020 that this trend could reverse.

Income

Despite the economic crash in 2008–2009, growth in the world's economic output continued to outpace growth in its population. But then came the impact on trade, jobs, and incomes of Covid-19.

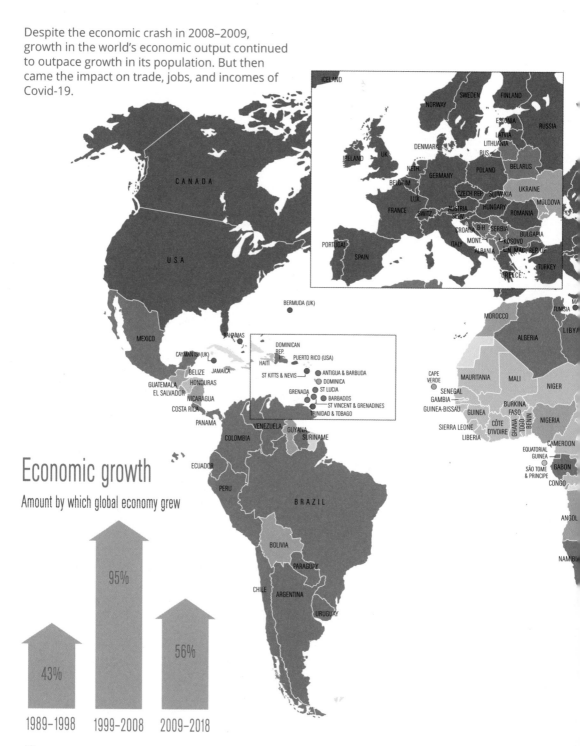

ICELAND
NORWAY SWEDEN FINLAND
ESTONIA RUSSIA
LATVIA
DENMARK LITHUANIA
IRELAND UK RUS.
NETH BELARUS
BELGIUM GERMANY POLAND
LUX. CZECH REP. SLOVAKIA UKRAINE
FRANCE AUSTRIA HUNGARY MOLDOVA
SWITZ. SLOV. ROMANIA
CROATIA B-H SERBIA BULGARIA
ITALY MONT. KOSOVO
PORTUGAL ALBANIA N. MAC. REP. OF
SPAIN GREECE TURKEY

CANADA

U.S.A

MEXICO

BERMUDA (UK)

BAHAMAS
CAYMAN IS. (UK)
BELIZE JAMAICA
GUATEMALA HONDURAS
EL SALVADOR
NICARAGUA
COSTA RICA
PANAMA

DOMINICAN REP.
HAITI PUERTO RICO (USA)
ST KITTS & NEVIS ANTIGUA & BARBUDA
DOMINICA
GRENADA ST LUCIA
BARBADOS
ST VINCENT & GRENADINES
TRINIDAD & TOBAGO

VENEZUELA GUYANA
COLOMBIA SURINAME
ECUADOR

PERU
BRAZIL

BOLIVIA
PARAGUAY
CHILE ARGENTINA
URUGUAY

TUNISIA
MOROCCO
ALGERIA LIBYA

CAPE VERDE MAURITANIA MALI NIGER
SENEGAL BURKINA
GAMBIA FASO NIGERIA
GUINEA-BISSAU GUINEA CÔTE TOGO BENIN
SIERRA LEONE D'IVOIRE GHANA
LIBERIA CAMEROON
EQUATORIAL GUINEA
SÃO TOMÉ GABON
& PRÍNCIPE CONGO

ANGOLA

NAMIBIA

Economic growth

Amount by which global economy grew

43%
1989–1998

95%
1999–2008

56%
2009–2018

Gross National Income

Per capita

2016 or latest available data

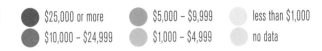

- $25,000 or more
- $10,000 – $24,999
- $5,000 – $9,999
- $1,000 – $4,999
- less than $1,000
- no data

RUSSIA

KAZAKHSTAN

MONGOLIA

UZBEKISTAN

GEORGIA

KYRGYZSTAN

JAPAN

ARMENIA   AZER.   TURKMEN.

SOUTH
KOREA

TAJIKISTAN

CYPRUS
LEB.

ISRAEL

IRAQ

IRAN

AFGHANISTAN

CHINA

PALESTINE   JORDAN

KUWAIT

BHUTAN

MACAO SAR (CHINA)

TAIWAN

BAHRAIN

QATAR

PAKISTAN

NEPAL

HONG KONG SAR (CHINA)

EGYPT

U.A.E.

SAUDI
ARABIA

BANGLADESH

OMAN

INDIA

MYANMAR

LAOS

CHAD

SUDAN

ERITREA   YEMEN

THAILAND

PHILIPPINES

VIETNAM

CAMBODIA

C.A.R.

SOUTH
SUDAN

ETHIOPIA

SRI LANKA

MALDIVES

BRUNEI

UGANDA

KENYA

MALAYSIA

D.R.
CONGO

RWANDA

SINGAPORE

BURUNDI

TANZANIA

SEYCHELLES

INDONESIA

PAPUA
NEW
GUINEA

SOLOMON
ISLANDS

COMOROS

TIMOR-LESTE

ZAMBIA   MALAWI

MADAGASCAR

ZIMBABWE

MAURITIUS

BOTSWANA

MOZAMBIQUE

SOUTH
AFRICA

SWAZILAND

AUSTRALIA

LESOTHO

NEW
ZEALAND

MICRONESIA, FED. ST. OF

MARSHALL ISLANDS

PALAU

NAURU

KIRIBATI

TUVALU

SAMOA

VANUATU

FIJI

TONGA

Inequality

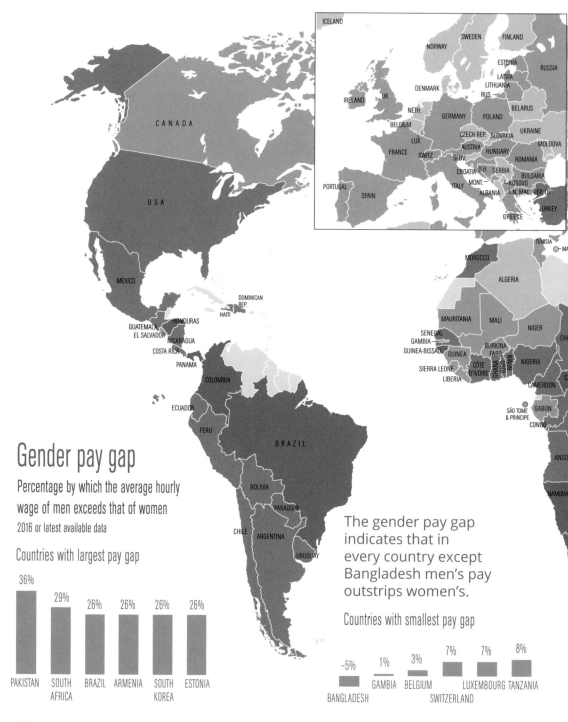

Gender pay gap

Percentage by which the average hourly wage of men exceeds that of women

2016 or latest available data

Countries with largest pay gap

36%	29%	26%	26%	26%	26%
PAKISTAN	SOUTH AFRICA	BRAZIL	ARMENIA	SOUTH KOREA	ESTONIA

The gender pay gap indicates that in every country except Bangladesh men's pay outstrips women's.

Countries with smallest pay gap

–5%	1%	3%	7%	7%	8%
BANGLADESH	GAMBIA	BELGIUM	SWITZERLAND	LUXEMBOURG	TANZANIA

Distribution of wealth

Within a country

2017 or latest available data
Gini index

50 – 63 *most unequal*

40 – 49

30 – 39

22 – 29 *most equal*

no data

The Gini index measures the degree to which the distribution of wealth within a country is different from a perfectly equal distribution.

World poverty

Percentage of population
living on less than $1.90 a day

2017 or latest available data
PPP$

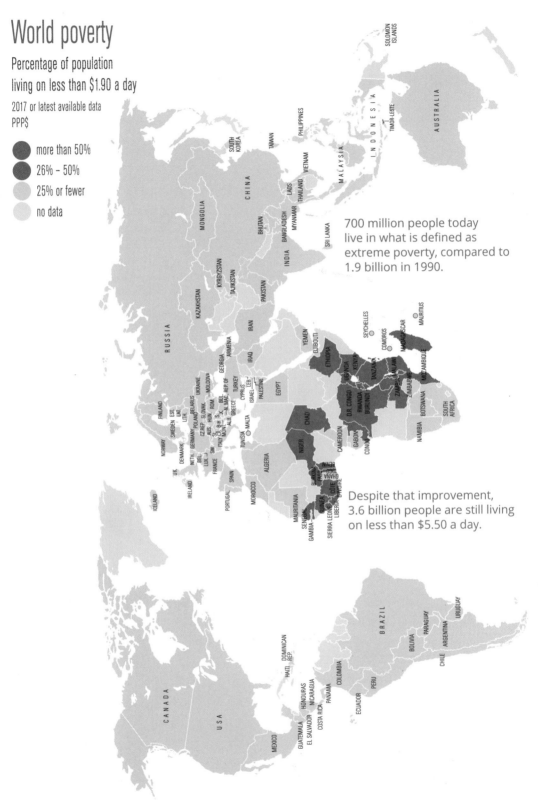

- more than 50%
- 26% – 50%
- 25% or fewer
- no data

700 million people today
live in what is defined as
extreme poverty, compared to
1.9 billion in 1990.

Despite that improvement,
3.6 billion people are still living
on less than $5.50 a day.

46

The hands of a few

Countries with the most billionaires in 2019

👤 10 billionaires 2009   👤 10 billionaires 2019

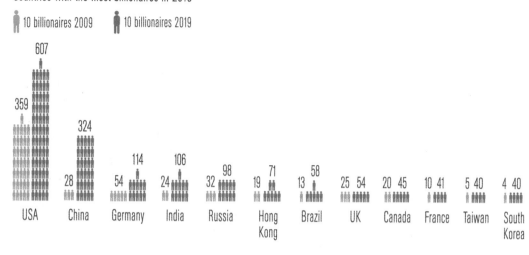

USA	China	Germany	India	Russia	Hong Kong	Brazil	UK	Canada	France	Taiwan	South Korea
359 / 607	28 / 324	54 / 114	24 / 106	32 / 98	19 / 71	13 / 58	25 / 54	20 / 45	10 / 41	5 / 40	4 / 40

Bouncing back

Number of billionaires and their total wealth
2008–2019

Billionaires were hit hard by the global crash in 2008. They recovered quickly.

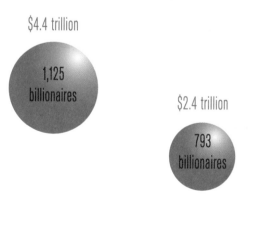

$4.4 trillion
1,125 billionaires
2008

$2.4 trillion
793 billionaires
2009

$8.7 trillion
2,153 billionaires
2019

Quality of life

There is more to happiness than wealth alone – yet rich countries inevitably offer a higher quality of life.

ICELAND
NORWAY
SWEDEN
FINLAND
ESTONIA
RUSSIA
LATVIA
DENMARK
LITHUANIA
RUS.
IRELAND
UK
NETH.
GERMANY
POLAND
BELARUS
BELGIUM
LUX.
LIECHT.
CZECH REP.
SLOVAKIA
UKRAINE
FRANCE
SWITZ.
AUSTRIA
HUNGARY
MOLDOVA
SLOV.
ROMANIA
PORTUGAL
ANDORRA
CROATIA
B-H
SERBIA
BULGARIA
MONT.
SPAIN
ITALY
ALBANIA
L-N. MAC. REP. OF
ALBANIA
TURKEY
GREECE

CANADA

USA

MEXICO

CUBA

BAHAMAS

DOMINICAN REP.

HAITI

ST KITTS & NEVIS
ANTIGUA & BARBUDA
ST VINCENT & GRENADINES
DOMINICA
ST LUCIA
GRENADA
BARBADOS

BELIZE
JAMAICA
GUATEMALA
HONDURAS
EL SALVADOR
NICARAGUA
COSTA RICA
PANAMA

TRINIDAD & TOBAGO

VENEZUELA
GUYANA
COLOMBIA
SURINAME

ECUADOR

PERU

BRAZIL

BOLIVIA

PARAGUAY

CHILE
ARGENTINA

URUGUAY

TUNISIA
MA

MOROCCO
ALGERIA
LIBYA

CAPE VERDE
MAURITANIA
MALI
NIGER

SENEGAL
GAMBIA
GUINEA-BISSAU
GUINEA
BURKINA FASO
NIGERIA
SIERRA LEONE
GHANA
TOGO
BENIN
LIBERIA
CAMEROON

SÃO TOME & PRINCIPE
CONGO

CÔTE D'IVOIRE

GABON
ANG

EQUATORIAL GUINEA

NAMIE

4 of the highest
CO$_2$ emitters
are also among
the top 20 countries
with the highest HDI

Relative human development

Score on the Human Development Index (HDI)

2017

- very high
- high
- medium
- low
- no data

The Human Development Index (HDI) scores countries according to the life expectancy and educational level of their populations, and the national income per capita.

Wealth for wellbeing?

HDI ranking much lower than Gross National Income ranking.

This suggests a country uses less than the average proportion of national wealth to improve the quality of life of its citizens.

Transnationals

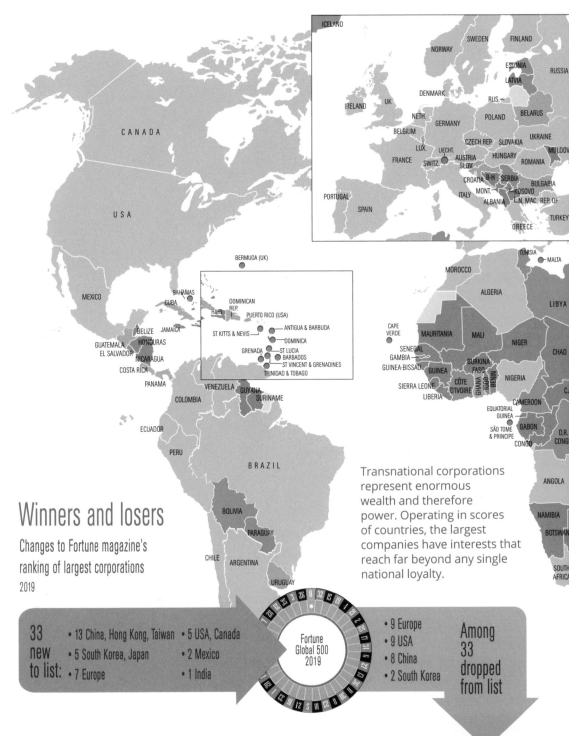

Transnational corporations represent enormous wealth and therefore power. Operating in scores of countries, the largest companies have interests that reach far beyond any single national loyalty.

Winners and losers

Changes to Fortune magazine's ranking of largest corporations
2019

33 new to list:
- 13 China, Hong Kong, Taiwan
- 5 South Korea, Japan
- 7 Europe
- 5 USA, Canada
- 2 Mexico
- 1 India

Fortune Global 500 2019

- 9 Europe
- 9 USA
- 8 China
- 2 South Korea

Among 33 dropped from list

Corporate wealth exceeds country wealth

Gross National Income (GNI) compared with annual revenue of selected transnationals

2017/18 or latest available GNI data
US$

- GNI larger than revenue of any company
- GNI smaller than Walmart ($500bn)
- GNI smaller than Boeing ($93bn)
- GNI smaller than Facebook ($41bn)
- GNI smaller than McDonalds ($23bn)
- no data

Comparing countries' Gross National Income (GNI) with the revenue of some of the giants of the corporate world is salutary. The largest corporation is Walmart. Only 24 countries have a GNI larger than its revenue, and nearly 90 sovereign states and dependencies have populations smaller than Walmart's global workforce of 2.2 million.

Banks

Comparative wealth

Gross National Income (GNI) compared with JPMorgan Chase
annual revenue of $131.4bn

2017–2018 or latest available date
for GNI

GNI greater than annual revenue of JPMorgan Chase

GNI smaller than annual revenue of JPMorgan Chase

GNI smaller than annual revenue of JPMorgan Chase
as is the combined GNI of these 48 countries

no data

RUSSIA

KAZAKHSTAN

MONGOLIA

JAPAN

UZBEKISTAN

KYRGYZSTAN

GEORGIA

SOUTH
KOREA

ARMENIA AZER. TURKMEN.

TAJIKISTAN

MICRONESIA, FED. ST. OF
MARSHALL ISLANDS
PALAU
NAURU

CYPRUS LEB.
ISRAEL

SYRIA

AFGHANISTAN

CHINA

KIRIBATI

IRAQ

IRAN

TUVALU

JORDAN

PALESTINE

KUWAIT

PAKISTAN

NEPAL

BHUTAN

BAHRAIN QATAR

MACAO SAR (CHINA)

SAMOA

U.A.E.

HONG KONG SAR (CHINA)

EGYPT

SAUDI
ARABIA

BANGLADESH

OMAN

INDIA

MYANMAR

LAOS

VANUATU

FIJI

SUDAN

ERITREA YEMEN

THAILAND

PHILIPPINES

VIETNAM

DJIBOUTI

CAMBODIA

TONGA

SOUTH
SUDAN

ETHIOPIA

SRI LANKA

BRUNEI

D.R.
CONGO

UGANDA

SOMALIA

MALDIVES

MALAYSIA

KENYA

SINGAPORE

RWANDA

BURUNDI

SEYCHELLES

TANZANIA

INDONESIA

PAPUA
NEW
GUINEA

SOLOMON
ISLANDS

COMOROS

TIMOR-LESTE

ZAMBIA

MALAWI

ZIMBABWE

MADAGASCAR

MAURITIUS

OTSWANA

MOZAMBIQUE

Weighed in the balance…

2017–2018

AUSTRALIA

SOUTH
AFRICA

SWAZILAND

LESOTHO

$131bn

$124bn

Combined GNI of the 48
countries with lowest GNI

JPMorgan Chase
revenue

NEW
ZEALAND

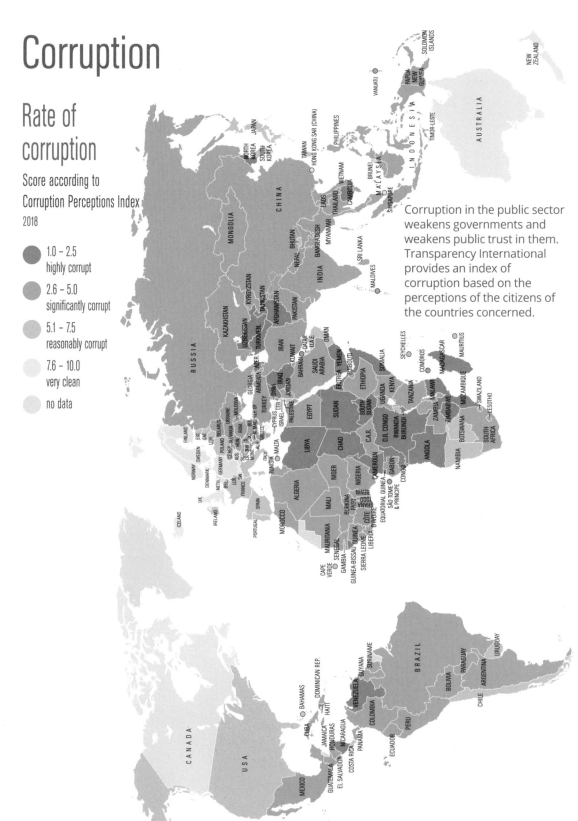

Corruption

Rate of corruption

Score according to
Corruption Perceptions Index
2018

- 1.0 – 2.5
  highly corrupt
- 2.6 – 5.0
  significantly corrupt
- 5.1 – 7.5
  reasonably corrupt
- 7.6 – 10.0
  very clean
- no data

Corruption in the public sector weakens governments and weakens public trust in them. Transparency International provides an index of corruption based on the perceptions of the citizens of the countries concerned.

Shadow economy

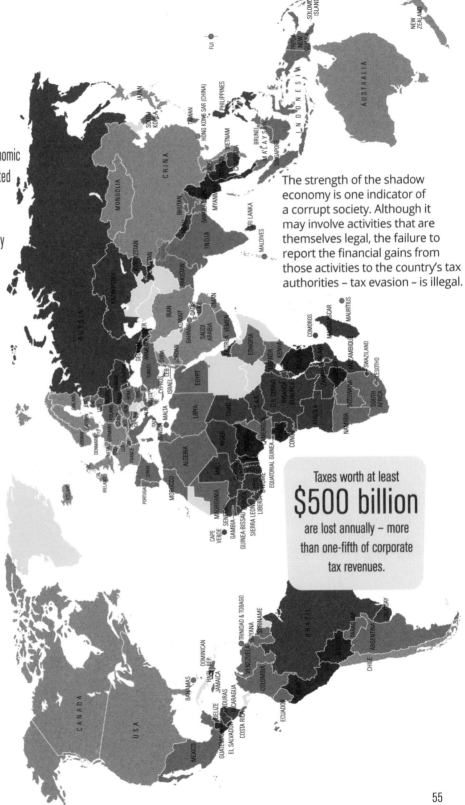

Value of legal economic activities unreported to authorities as percentage of formal economy

average of 2004–15

- 51% – 67%
- 36% – 50%
- 21% – 35%
- 7% – 20%
- no data

The strength of the shadow economy is one indicator of a corrupt society. Although it may involve activities that are themselves legal, the failure to report the financial gains from those activities to the country's tax authorities – tax evasion – is illegal.

Taxes worth at least
$500 billion
are lost annually – more than one-fifth of corporate tax revenues.

Panama and Paradise Papers

The Panama Papers are the biggest ever text dump in history – the result not of hacking but of a leak from an anonymous source. It offered up for global public scrutiny internal documents of Mossack Fonseca, a Panama-based law firm specializing in "offshore services" for rich individuals and corporate clients. The core of the service is how best to hide money from tax authorities. The following year came the Paradise Papers, a similar leak, with documents from three companies, headquartered in Bermuda and Singapore.

The global trade in offshore financial services is not a minor or marginal part of the world's economic and financial system. It is at the core of it. What the two document dumps revealed is that many of the world's political and corporate leaders, celebrities and stars, and people closely connected to them have turned to this industry to handle their wealth.

The essence of democracy is transparency and accountability: we see what governments do and every few years we hold them to account in an election. The essence of the offshore financial services sector is the very opposite. They keep their work secret and are accountable to nobody but their clients as they move legitimately earned (or inherited) wealth outside any national system of regulation or taxation.

The heart of the story revealed by the leaks is a struggle between governments that want tax income to fund vital public services, and rich individuals who don't want to provide it. The latter are aided by individuals, companies and a few governments that profit from the trade in non-accountability and opacity.

Scale of the leaks

Panama Papers

2.6 terabytes   **11.5m** files

Paradise Papers

1.4 terabytes   **13.4m** files

The struggle is an unequal one, and not just because powerful people in countries that need tax income are among those who use offshore financial services. The struggle is unequal because states and governments have borders and, in the modern world, money does not. For the rich, it is easy to move money outside the scope of government regulation and oversight, into a quiet, safe place – a haven – calling on it when needed. But the scrutiny the offshore trade has come under since 2016 has made the havens less comfortable.

Offshore financial services

Top ten providers based on number of companies registered there
that appeared in Mossack Fonseca's files (Panama Papers)
1977–2015

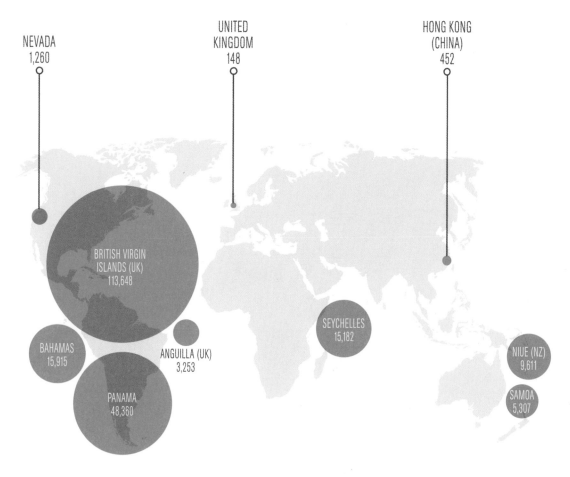

NEVADA
1,260

UNITED
KINGDOM
148

HONG KONG
(CHINA)
452

BRITISH VIRGIN
ISLANDS (UK)
113,648

BAHAMAS
15,915

ANGUILLA (UK)
3,253

PANAMA
48,360

SEYCHELLES
15,182

NIUE (NZ)
9,611

SAMOA
5,307

Many companies are no more than convenient fictions to hide money. In the Caribbean island of Nevis, population 11,000, there are more than 18,000 registered companies. There are individuals elsewhere in the region who are on the books as directors or company secretaries to thousands of firms.

These fictions are not the speciality of the Caribbean alone. In a smart street in London, one address is the registered HQ of over 2,000 companies. Few of them use the building for office space. One company that does is in the business of creating other companies. It has brought into existence over 10 million companies.

Panama and Paradise – power players

Country to which individual named in Panama Papers (1977–2016)
and Paradise Papers (1950–2016) had political links

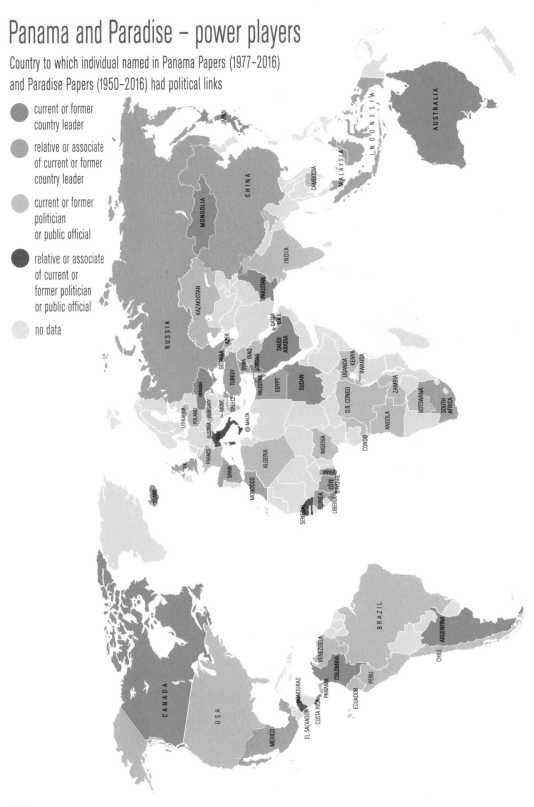

- current or former
  country leader
- relative or associate
  of current or former
  country leader
- current or former
  politician
  or public official
- relative or associate
  of current or
  former politician
  or public official
- no data

Panama Papers – effects of leak

as of March 2019

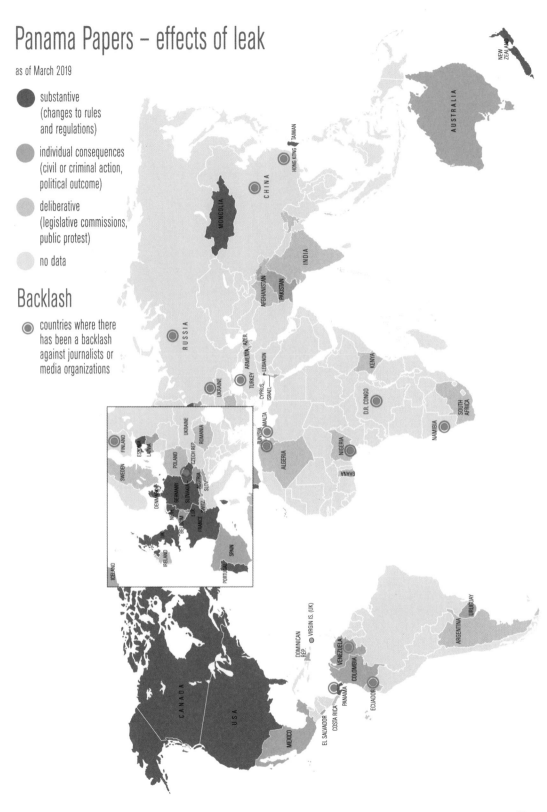

substantive
(changes to rules
and regulations)

individual consequences
(civil or criminal action,
political outcome)

deliberative
(legislative commissions,
public protest)

no data

Backlash

countries where there
has been a backlash
against journalists or
media organizations

NEW ZEALAND

AUSTRALIA

TAIWAN
HONG KONG

CHINA

MONGOLIA

INDIA

AFGHANISTAN
PAKISTAN

RUSSIA

ARMENIA AZER.
TURKEY
LEBANON
CYPRUS
ISRAEL

UKRAINE

KENYA

D.R. CONGO

SOUTH AFRICA

NAMIBIA

UKRAINE
ROMANIA
TUNISIA MALTA
FINLAND
ESTONIA
LATVIA
SWEDEN
POLAND
CZECH REP.
AUSTRIA
SLOVAKIA SLOV.
DENMARK
GERMANY
NETH.
SWITZ.
BELGIUM
FRANCE
LUX.
UK
IRELAND
ICELAND
PORTUGAL
SPAIN

ALGERIA

NIGERIA

GHANA

URUGUAY

ARGENTINA

DOMINICAN REP.
VIRGIN IS. (UK)

VENEZUELA

COLOMBIA

PANAMA

ECUADOR

CANADA

U.S.A.

MEXICO

EL SALVADOR
COSTA RICA

59

Debt

Government debt

Gross debt as
a percentage of GDP
2018

- 150% or more
- 100% – 149%
- 50% – 99%
- less than 50%
- no data

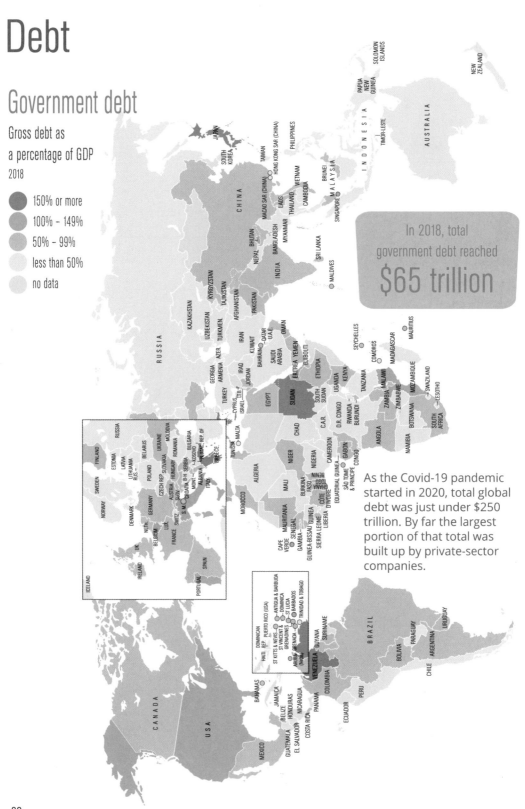

In 2018, total
government debt reached
$65 trillion

As the Covid-19 pandemic
started in 2020, total global
debt was just under $250
trillion. By far the largest
portion of that total was
built up by private-sector
companies.

Household debt

Private debt, loans, and debt securities as percentage of GDP

2017

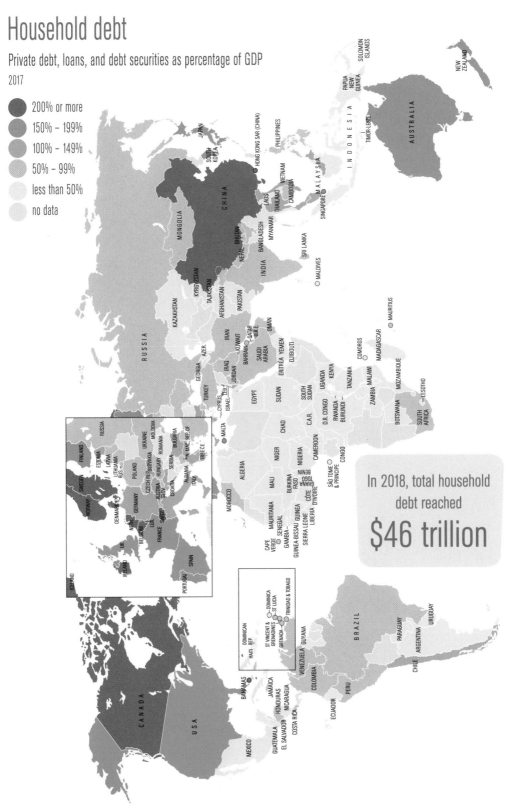

200% or more

150% – 199%

100% – 149%

50% – 99%

less than 50%

no data

In 2018, total household debt reached

$46 trillion

How the money's made

The route to a sophisticated modern economy passes from agriculture, to mass-production industry, to hi-tech manufacture, and finally to knowledge and services.

Tourism dependency

Percentage contribution made to GDP by income from tourism

2018
Selected countries

Maldives 32%

Seychelles 27%

Bahamas 20%

Which sector dominates a country's economy?

Contribution to GDP at least 20% higher
than that of other sector(s)

2018 or latest available data

services

agricultural and services

agriculture

industry

industry and services

sectors within 20% of each other

no data

RUSSIA

KAZAKHSTAN

MONGOLIA

JAPAN

GEORGIA
ARMENIA   AZER.   UZBEKISTAN   KYRGYZSTAN
TURKMEN.   TAJIKISTAN

SOUTH
KOREA

CYPRUS   LEB.   IRAQ   AFGHANISTAN
ISRAEL
JORDAN   IRAN   CHINA

PALESTINE

EGYPT   KUWAIT   PAKISTAN   NEPAL   BHUTAN
BAHRAIN
QATAR   MACAO SAR (CHINA)
SAUDI   UAE
ARABIA   BANGLADESH   HONG KONG SAR (CHINA)
OMAN   INDIA
SUDAN   MYANMAR   LAOS

YEMEN   THAILAND   VIETNAM   PHILIPPINES

DJIBOUTI   CAMBODIA

SOUTH
SUDAN   ETHIOPIA   SRI LANKA

MALDIVES   BRUNEI

D.R.   UGANDA
CONGO   KENYA   MALAYSIA

RWANDA   SINGAPORE
BURUNDI   SEYCHELLES
TANZANIA

COMOROS   INDONESIA

ZAMBIA   MALAWI   TIMOR-LESTE

ZIMBABWE   MADAGASCAR
TSWANA   MAURITIUS

MOZAMBIQUE

SOUTH   SWAZILAND
AFRICA   LESOTHO   AUSTRALIA

MICRONESIA, FED. ST. OF
MARSHALL ISLANDS
PALAU
NAURU
KIRIBATI

FIJI

NEW
ZEALAND

Rights and respect

Protection from both economic depredation and the threat of violent conflicts derives from laws made for the common good. When laws are made by a process that represents and responds to the interests of the majority, and are accepted rather than imposed, then social order is based on the rule of law and the contract between citizen and state upholds accountable authority. Such societies are more resilient, and the majority of people fare better, than when power is arbitrary and laws are made by an elite minority for their own interests.

Ours is an age of growing democracy – at least when measured by the number of countries that are now established democracies, and the percentage of the world population that lives in them. This is a relatively new development. The world has only been moving in that direction for one or two centuries, and until the last 20 to 30 years democratic government was not the global norm.

The transition from dictatorship to democracy is perilous. Those who expect to be disadvantaged by that transition almost always resist the change if they can. It is hard to end the ensuing conflict peacefully when the institutions that might keep it peaceful are themselves being fought over. The democratic wave that swept the Middle East in 2011 and 2012 was accompanied everywhere by violence, with open civil war in Libya and Syria.

Once a democracy is established that is not always the whole story. In Europe, Asia, and the Americas, democracies have witnessed a fragmentation of political norms and social consensus in the past decade. The trend is not uniform but it is real, and where it unfolds it weakens democracy. In large part, it results from economic problems and feeds on a slow erosion of democracy's vitality. In many established democracies, despite surges of political energy on issues such as the climate crisis, political participation is not high. Voting is as far as most citizens' political participation goes, and even then a large turnout cannot always be counted on.

In 2020, the emergency measures required to meet the challenge of the Covid-19 pandemic were used by some governments to restrict political freedoms. It is a tragic irony that this will weaken their countries' ability to bounce back from the effects of the pandemic and other major shocks.

Political systems

GREENLAND (Den)

ICELAND   FAROE IS. (Den)

NORWAY   SWEDE

CANADA

DENMARK
IRELAND   UK   POLA
NETH.   GERMANY
BEL   LIECHT.   CZ RE
LUX   AUS
FRANCE   SW   SL
ITALY   CR
MONACO   MONT
ALB

USA

PORTUGAL   SPAIN

TUNISIA

MONACO

BERMUDA (UK)

MOROCCO

WESTERN
SAHARA (Mor.)   ALGERIA   LIBY

MEXICO   BAHAMAS

CUBA   CAPE   MAURITANIA   MALI   NIGER
CAYMAN IS. (UK)   VERDE
BELIZE   DOM. REP.   SENEGAL   CH
JAMAICA   HAITI   PUERTO RICO (USA)   GAMBIA   BURKINA
GUATEMALA   HONDURAS   ST K. & N.   ANT. & BARB.   GUINEA-BISSAU   GUINEA   FASO   BENIN
EL SALVADOR   GUADELOUPE (Fr)   CÔTE   GHANA   NIGERIA
NICARAGUA   DOM.   MARTINIQUE (Fr)   SIERRA LEONE   TOGO
NETH. ANT.   GRENADA   ST LUCIA   D'IVOIRE
COSTA RICA   BARBADOS   LIBERIA   CAMEROON
PANAMA   ST VINCENT & GREN.   EQUATORIAL
VENEZUELA   TR. & TOB.   GUINEA   GABON
GUYANA   SÃO TOME   CONGO
& PRINCIPE

Living politics

Number of people living under
different political systems ↗➤
2019

COLOMBIA   SURINAME
FRENCH GUIANA (Fr)

ECUADOR

PERU

BRAZIL

ANGOLA

👤 10 million people

3,679m

BOLIVIA

NAMIBI

PARAGUAY

1,983m

CHILE   ARGENTINA

1,820m

152m

URUGUAY

FALKLANDS IS. (UK)

established
democracy

effective or formal
one-party rule

weak, uncertain, or
transitional democracy

monarchy or
theocracy

Current political systems

2019

● established democracy

● effective or formal one-party rule

● state of disorder

● weak, uncertain, or transitional democracy

● monarchy or theocracy

● dependent territory

FINLAND

RUSSIA

BELARUS

UKRAINE

SKIA

MOLDOVA

ROM.

BUL.

N.MAC.

K.

REP. OF

ECE

GEORGIA

KAZAKHSTAN

MONGOLIA

TURKEY

ARMENIA

AZER.

UZBEKISTAN

KYRGYZSTAN

TURKMEN.

TAJIKISTAN

NORTH
KOREA

JAPAN

N. CYPRUS (Turk)

CYPRUS

LEB.

SYRIA

ISRAEL

IRAQ

IRAN

AFGHANISTAN

CHINA

SOUTH
KOREA

PALESTINE

JORDAN

KUWAIT

PAKISTAN

BHUTAN

TAIWAN

BAHRAIN

QATAR

U.A.E.

NEPAL

EGYPT

SAUDI
ARABIA

OMAN

INDIA

BANGLADESH

MYANMAR

LAOS

PHILIPPINES

SUDAN

ERITREA

YEMEN

THAILAND

VIETNAM

DJIBOUTI

CAMBODIA

C.A.R.

SOUTH
SUDAN

ETHIOPIA

SRI LANKA

BRUNEI

UGANDA

SOMALIA

MALDIVES

MALAYSIA

D.R.
CONGO

KENYA

SINGAPORE

RWANDA

BURUNDI

SEYCHELLES

INDONESIA

TANZANIA

PAPUA
NEW
GUINEA

COMOROS

SOLOMON
ISLANDS

ZAMBIA

MALAWI

MADAGASCAR

TIMOR-LESTE

ZIMBABWE

MAURITIUS

BOTSWANA

MOZAMBIQUE

AUSTRALIA

SWAZILAND

LESOTHO

MICRONESIA, FED. ST. OF

MARSHALL IS.

PALAU

NAURU

KIRIBATI

TUVALU

SAMOA

VANUATU

FIJI

COOK IS. (NZ)

TONGA

NEW CALEDONIA (Fr)

FRENCH POLYNESIA (Fr)

In **2019**,
for the first time,
there were
**no military
dictatorships**

NEW
ZEALAND

62m

ⵎⵎⵎⵎⵎ

state of
disorder

6m

dependent
territory

Transition to and from democracy

Most recent transition to weak or established democracy
with universal suffrage

2019

Suffrage for all men
over 21 and women
over 30 years
1918
Equal suffrage
for both sexes
1928

Norway
Full male suffrage
1898
Female suffrage
1913

Belgium
Full male suffrage 1918
Female suffrage 1948

Switzerland
Full male suffrage
1848
Female suffrage
1971

France
Full male suffrage
1848
Female suffrage
1944

Canada
Suffrage for men
and women 1918
First Nations
people able to
vote without
losing Indian
status and treaty
rights 1960

USA
Full White male
suffrage 1856
Full White female
suffrage 1920
Suffrage for all Native
Americans 1957
Universal suffrage,
including for all African
Americans 1965

CANADA

USA

MEXICO

BELIZE
GUATEMALA
HONDURAS
EL SALVADOR
NICARAGUA
COSTA RICA
PANAMA

BAHAMAS
CUBA
HAITI
JAMAICA

ST KITTS & NEVIS

DOMINICAN
REP.

ANTIGUA & BARBUDA
DOMINICA
GRENADA
ST LUCIA
BARBADOS
ST VINCENT & GRENADINES
TRINIDAD & TOBAGO

VENEZUELA
COLOMBIA
ECUADOR
PERU

GUYANA
SURINAME

BRAZIL

BOLIVIA
PARAGUAY
CHILE
ARGENTINA
URUGUAY

ICELAND

NORWAY
IRELAND
UK
FRANCE
PORTUGAL
SPAIN

SWEDEN
DENMARK
NETH.
GERMANY
LIECHT.
LUX.
MONACO

LI
POL
CZ REP.
AUS.
SL
CR B
MONT.
ITALY
TUNISIA
MA

MOROCCO

ALGERIA

LIBYA

CAPE
VERDE
SENEGAL
GAMBIA
GUINEA-BISSAU

MAURITANIA

MALI

NIGER

CH

GUINEA
SIERRA LEONE
LIBERIA
CÔTE
D'IVOIRE
GHANA
TOGO
BENIN

BURKINA
FASO

NIGERIA

CA

EQUATORIAL
GUINEA
SÃO TOME
& PRINCIPE
CONGO

CAMEROON

GABON

ANGO

NAMIBL

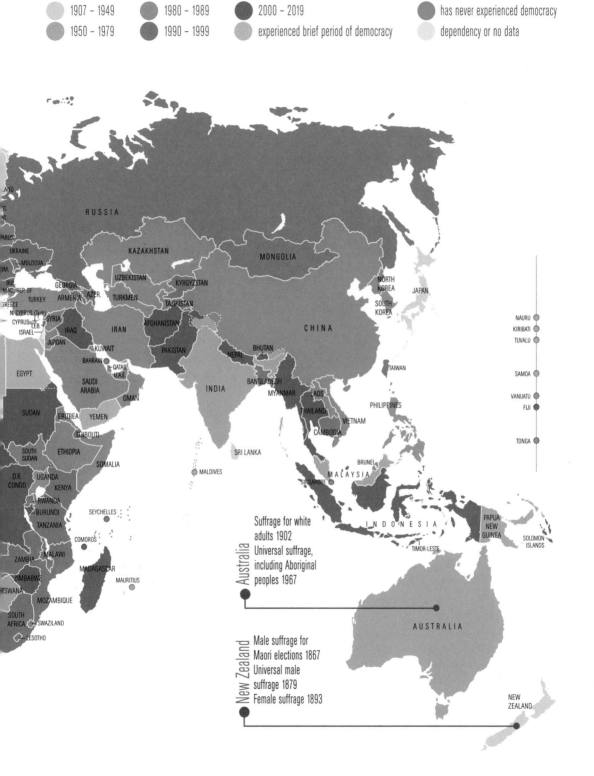

1907 – 1949
1950 – 1979
1980 – 1989
1990 – 1999
2000 – 2019
experienced brief period of democracy
has never experienced democracy
dependency or no data

RUSSIA

KAZAKHSTAN

MONGOLIA

UKRAINE
MOLDOVA

BUL.
MAC. REP. OF
GREECE TURKEY
N. CYPRUS (Turk.)
CYPRUS LEB.
ISRAEL

GEORGIA
ARMENIA AZER.
TURKMEN.

UZBEKISTAN
KYRGYZSTAN
TAJIKISTAN

AFGHANISTAN

NORTH
KOREA
SOUTH
KOREA

JAPAN

SYRIA
IRAQ
JORDAN
KUWAIT
BAHRAIN QATAR
U.A.E.

IRAN

CHINA

TAIWAN

NAURU
KIRIBATI
TUVALU

EGYPT

SAUDI
ARABIA
OMAN

PAKISTAN

NEPAL BHUTAN

INDIA
BANGLADESH
MYANMAR

SAMOA

VANUATU
FIJI

SUDAN
ERITREA YEMEN
DJIBOUTI

LAOS
THAILAND
VIETNAM
CAMBODIA

PHILIPPINES

TONGA

SOUTH
SUDAN
ETHIOPIA

SOMALIA

SRI LANKA

MALDIVES

D.R.
CONGO UGANDA
KENYA

RWANDA
BURUNDI
TANZANIA

SEYCHELLES

BRUNEI
MALAYSIA
SINGAPORE

INDONESIA

PAPUA
NEW
GUINEA
SOLOMON
ISLANDS

COMOROS

TIMOR-LESTE

ZAMBIA MALAWI
MADAGASCAR

ZIMBABWE
TSWANA

MAURITIUS

Suffrage for white
adults 1902
Universal suffrage,
including Aboriginal
peoples 1967

Australia

MOZAMBIQUE

SOUTH
AFRICA SWAZILAND
LESOTHO

AUSTRALIA

New Zealand

Male suffrage for
Maori elections 1867
Universal male
suffrage 1879
Female suffrage 1893

NEW
ZEALAND

Religious rights

Faith is often a matter of government policy, and in some countries is the cornerstone of the state. Almost a quarter of the world's states have a formal link to a religion enshrined in their constitution or laws. What this means in practice varies widely.

An official religion can mean intolerance, discrimination, or repression for other faiths – but a state-backed religion has also proved to be compatible with secularism in the state and tolerance in society. The greatest intolerance and violence can spring from religious groups that are, or were at one time, marginalized by the state.

CANADA

USA

MEXICO

CUBA

DOMINICAN REP

BELIZE   JAMAICA   HAITI

GUATEMALA   HONDURAS

EL SALVADOR

NICARAGUA   GRENADA   BARBADOS

COSTA RICA   TRINIDAD & TOBAGO

VENEZUELA

PANAMA

GUYANA   SURINAME

COLOMBIA

ECUADOR

PERU

BRAZIL

BOLIVIA

PARAGUAY

CHILE   ARGENTINA

URUGUAY

Sharia

The Islamic system of law (Sharia) derives from four sources – the Quran, accounts of the life of the Prophet, reasoning, and the established consensus of juridical opinion. It reaches more widely than Western ideas of law, and covers how to live virtuously as well as legal norms and crimes.

Sharia has largely been replaced by secular (Western) law in most countries, with the exception of family law. Towards the end of the 20th century, some movements and some governments in Islamic countries started to give increased weight to Sharia. Only two countries exclusively rely on it today.

State attitude towards religion

2018 or most recent available data

- ● discriminates against all religions
- ● favours religion of majority and interferes with others
- ● favours religion of majority, tolerates all others
- ● tolerates all religions
- ● no data
- • state religion established in law

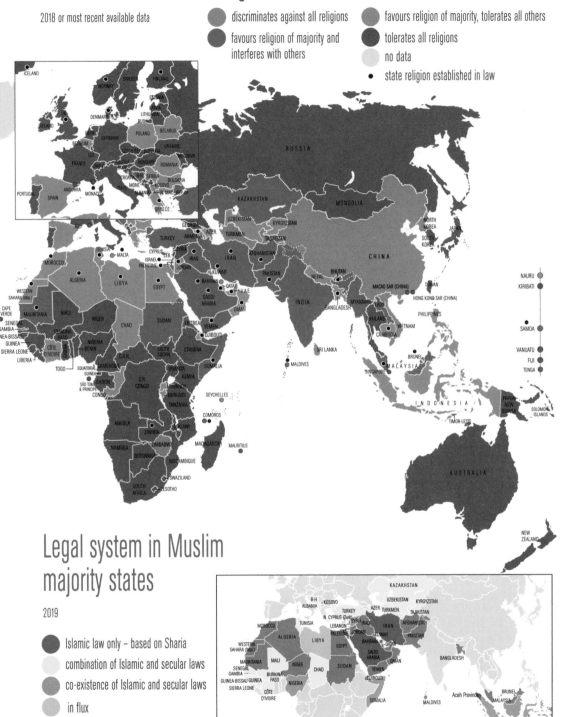

Legal system in Muslim majority states

2019

- ● Islamic law only – based on Sharia
- ● combination of Islamic and secular laws
- ● co-existence of Islamic and secular laws
- ● in flux
- ● secular law only

Human rights

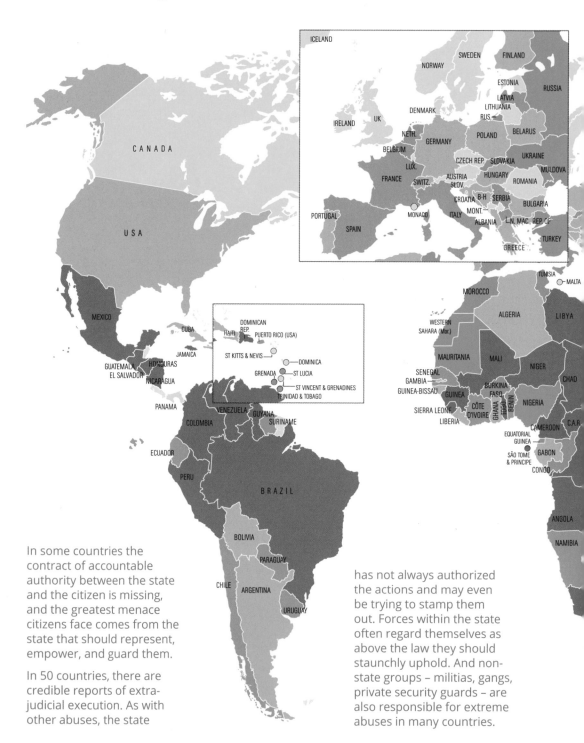

In some countries the contract of accountable authority between the state and the citizen is missing, and the greatest menace citizens face comes from the state that should represent, empower, and guard them.

In 50 countries, there are credible reports of extra-judicial execution. As with other abuses, the state has not always authorized the actions and may even be trying to stamp them out. Forces within the state often regard themselves as above the law they should staunchly uphold. And non-state groups – militias, gangs, private security guards – are also responsible for extreme abuses in many countries.

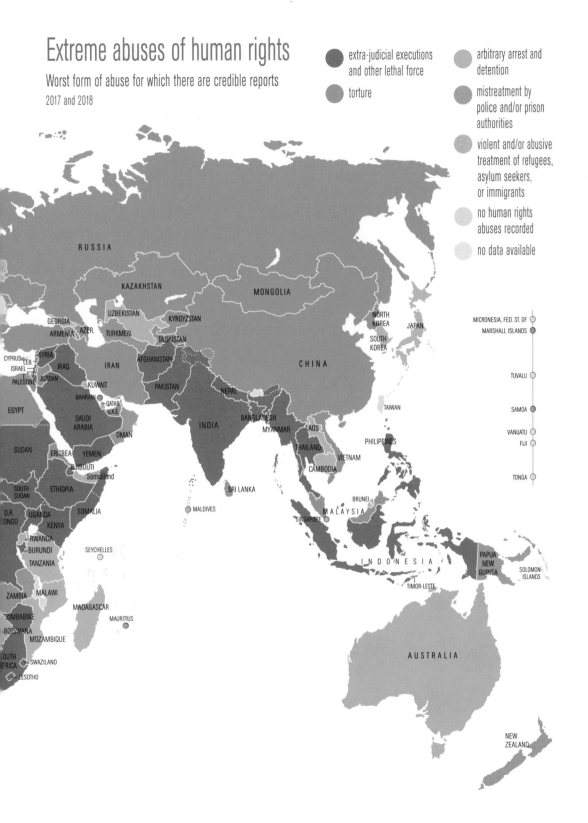

Extreme abuses of human rights

Worst form of abuse for which there are credible reports

2017 and 2018

extra-judicial executions and other lethal force

torture

arbitrary arrest and detention

mistreatment by police and/or prison authorities

violent and/or abusive treatment of refugees, asylum seekers, or immigrants

no human rights abuses recorded

no data available

RUSSIA

KAZAKHSTAN

MONGOLIA

GEORGIA

UZBEKISTAN

KYRGYZSTAN

ARMENIA   AZER.

TURKMEN.

TAJIKISTAN

NORTH KOREA

JAPAN

SOUTH KOREA

CYPRUS   LEB.

SYRIA

ISRAEL

IRAQ

IRAN

AFGHANISTAN

CHINA

PALESTINE   JORDAN

KUWAIT

PAKISTAN

NEPAL

BAHRAIN   QATAR

U.A.E.

EGYPT

SAUDI ARABIA

OMAN

INDIA

BANGLADESH

MYANMAR

LAOS

TAIWAN

SUDAN

ERITREA

YEMEN

THAILAND

VIETNAM

PHILIPPINES

DJIBOUTI

Somaliland

CAMBODIA

SOUTH SUDAN

ETHIOPIA

SRI LANKA

BRUNEI

D.R. CONGO

UGANDA

SOMALIA

MALDIVES

MALAYSIA

SINGAPORE

KENYA

RWANDA

BURUNDI

SEYCHELLES

I N D O N E S I A

PAPUA NEW GUINEA

TANZANIA

SOLOMON ISLANDS

TIMOR-LESTE

ZAMBIA

MALAWI

MADAGASCAR

ZIMBABWE

MAURITIUS

BOTSWANA

MOZAMBIQUE

AUSTRALIA

SOUTH AFRICA   SWAZILAND

LESOTHO

MICRONESIA, FED. ST. OF

MARSHALL ISLANDS

TUVALU

SAMOA

VANUATU

FIJI

TONGA

NEW ZEALAND

Judicial killings

Status of death penalty
As of 31 December 2018
USA, 2019

retentionist
retains death penalty for ordinary crimes

abolitionist for ordinary crimes only
law provides for death penalty only for exceptional crimes such as crimes under military law or crimes committed in exceptional circumstances

abolitionist in practice
retains death penalty for ordinary crimes such as murder but has not executed anyone during past 10 years and is believed to have a policy or established practice of not carrying out executions

abolitionist for all crimes
law does not provide for the death penalty for any crime

no data

The foundational idea of human rights is that there is something special and deserving of respect about every person.

Killing people, whether done according to that country's laws or illegally and arbitrarily, reveals an erosion of that respect.

Sex trafficking

Number of victims detected by police on
selected international and domestic routes
2014–2017

more than 1,000 people   301 – 1,000   151 – 300

USA

MEXICO

GUATEMALA
EL SALVADOR   HONDURAS

DOM. REP.

UK   DENMARK
NETH.
GERMANY   POLAND
CENT. & SE
FRANCE   HUN.   ROM
SPAIN   BULGARIA
ITALY

NIGERIA

SUB-SAHARAN AFRICA

BOLIVIA

ARGENTINA
URUGUAY

Honduras to USA Miguel, 14, was drugged and abducted by two men to the USA, where he was sold to traffickers and forced into sexual exploitation.

USA Taylor, 16, dated an older man who soon coerced her into prostitution, forcing her to make $1,000 a day at the age of 17, as well as recruiting more teenagers.

Romania to Germany A Romanian woman, 23, was offered an opportunity by a "friend" to marry a German. She travelled to Germany but found herself with no husband, in debt bondage to the "friend" and forced into prostitution. She now receives care from an NGO.

France Paul convinced his wife Adelaide to prostitute herself when they were in need of money. When she wanted to quit, he took her keys, phone, and money and forced her to continue, using psychological coercion and threats.

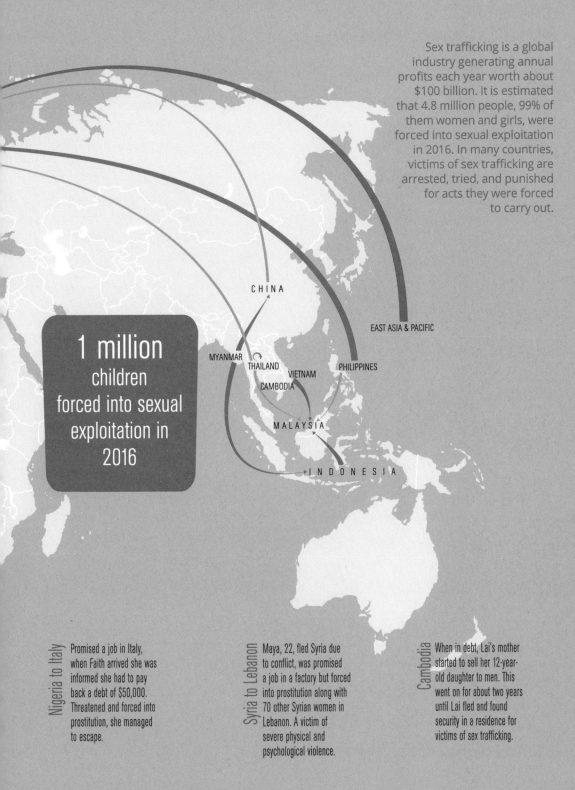

Sex trafficking is a global industry generating annual profits each year worth about $100 billion. It is estimated that 4.8 million people, 99% of them women and girls, were forced into sexual exploitation in 2016. In many countries, victims of sex trafficking are arrested, tried, and punished for acts they were forced to carry out.

CHINA

EAST ASIA & PACIFIC

MYANMAR
THAILAND
VIETNAM
PHILIPPINES
CAMBODIA

MALAYSIA

INDONESIA

1 million children forced into sexual exploitation in 2016

Nigeria to Italy
Promised a job in Italy, when Faith arrived she was informed she had to pay back a debt of $50,000. Threatened and forced into prostitution, she managed to escape.

Syria to Lebanon
Maya, 22, fled Syria due to conflict, was promised a job in a factory but forced into prostitution along with 70 other Syrian women in Lebanon. A victim of severe physical and psychological violence.

Cambodia
When in debt, Lai's mother started to sell her 12-year-old daughter to men. This went on for about two years until Lai fled and found security in a residence for victims of sex trafficking.

Children's rights

As with other groups, respect for the rights of children is steadily improving – yet that only throws into starker relief the abuses that continue. Too many children are not registered at birth, which deprives them of the rights and recognition of citizenship before they even get started in life.

Unregistered children

Unregistered births as percentage of all births

2018 or latest available data

70% or more
50% – 69%
30% – 49%
10% – 29%
19% or fewer
no data

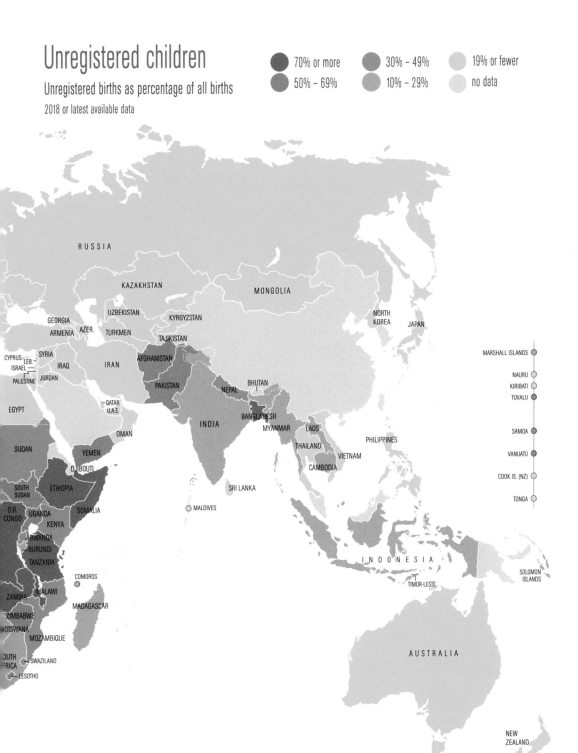

RUSSIA

KAZAKHSTAN

MONGOLIA

GEORGIA
ARMENIA AZER.
CYPRUS LEB.
ISRAEL
PALESTINE JORDAN
SYRIA
IRAQ
EGYPT

UZBEKISTAN
TURKMEN.
KYRGYZSTAN
TAJIKISTAN
IRAN
AFGHANISTAN
PAKISTAN
QATAR
U.A.E.
OMAN
YEMEN
DJIBOUTI

NORTH
KOREA
JAPAN

NEPAL
BHUTAN
INDIA
BANGLADESH
MYANMAR
LAOS
THAILAND
VIETNAM
CAMBODIA
PHILIPPINES

SRI LANKA

MALDIVES

SUDAN

SOUTH
SUDAN
D.R.
CONGO UGANDA
KENYA
RWANDA
BURUNDI
TANZANIA
ZAMBIA MALAWI
ZIMBABWE
OTSWANA
MOZAMBIQUE
OUTH
RICA SWAZILAND
LESOTHO
ETHIOPIA
SOMALIA

COMOROS

MADAGASCAR

INDONESIA

TIMOR-LESTE

SOLOMON
ISLANDS

AUSTRALIA

NEW
ZEALAND

MARSHALL ISLANDS
NAURU
KIRIBATI
TUVALU
SAMOA
VANUATU
COOK IS. (NZ)
TONGA

Children at work

Economically active children aged 5–17 years
as percentage of age-group
2019

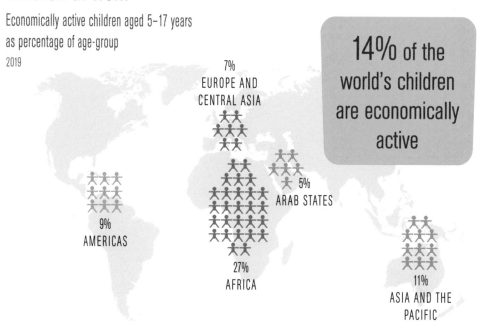

7%
EUROPE AND
CENTRAL ASIA

14% of the world's children are economically active

5%
ARAB STATES

9%
AMERICAS

27%
AFRICA

11%
ASIA AND THE
PACIFIC

Nearly one child in ten is economically active, and half of them are doing hazardous work, involving tasks that will cripple them in later years. Although the situation is improving, the rate of progress has slowed. Of those children aged 5 to 14 years who work, a third do not attend school.

Children at risk

Number of children employed in hazardous work

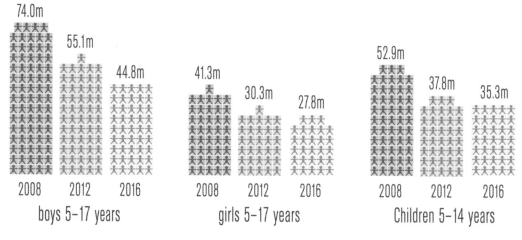

74.0m	55.1m	44.8m
2008	2012	2016

boys 5–17 years

41.3m	30.3m	27.8m
2008	2012	2016

girls 5–17 years

52.9m	37.8m	35.3m
2008	2012	2016

Children 5–14 years

Children not in school

Percentage of children of primary-school age not attending school by region
2017

● 1% in school
● 1% not in school

21%
Sub-Saharan Africa

15%
Arab World

7%
South Asia

6%
Middle East & North Africa

5%
Latin America & Caribbean

4%
North America

4%
East Asia & Pacific

3%
Europe & Central Asia

9%
World

Nearly one child in ten who should be attending primary school does not – more than 63 million absentees between the ages of 5 and 11.

Women's rights

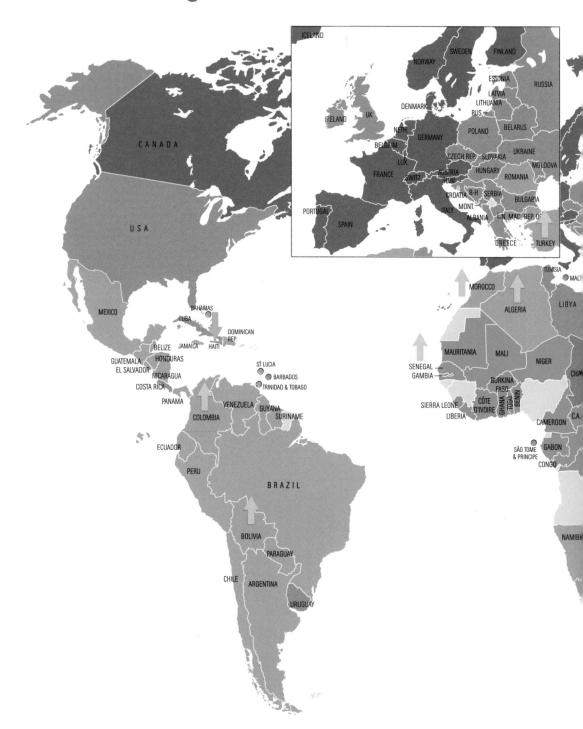

Equal rights

Gender Inequality Index score
2017

71 or more *least equal*

51 – 70

31 – 50

11 – 30

4 – 10 *most equal*

no data

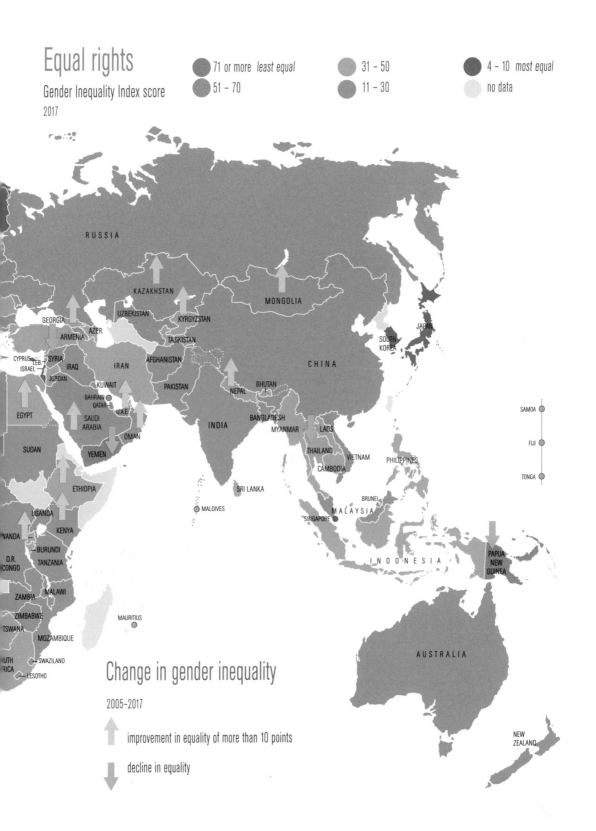

RUSSIA

KAZAKHSTAN

MONGOLIA

UZBEKISTAN

KYRGYZSTAN

GEORGIA

ARMENIA AZER.

TAJIKISTAN

JAPAN

SOUTH
KOREA

CYPRUS LEB. SYRIA

ISRAEL

JORDAN

IRAQ

IRAN

AFGHANISTAN

CHINA

KUWAIT

BAHRAIN QATAR

EGYPT

U.A.E.

SAUDI
ARABIA

OMAN

PAKISTAN

NEPAL

BHUTAN

INDIA

BANGLADESH

MYANMAR LAOS

SUDAN

YEMEN

THAILAND

VIETNAM

CAMBODIA

PHILIPPINES

SAMOA

FIJI

TONGA

ETHIOPIA

SRI LANKA

UGANDA

MALDIVES

BRUNEI

MALAYSIA

SINGAPORE

WANDA

KENYA

D.R.
CONGO

BURUNDI

TANZANIA

INDONESIA

PAPUA
NEW
GUINEA

ZAMBIA

MALAWI

ZIMBABWE

TSWANA

MAURITIUS

MOZAMBIQUE

UTH
RICA

SWAZILAND

LESOTHO

AUSTRALIA

Change in gender inequality

2005–2017

improvement in equality of more than 10 points

decline in equality

NEW
ZEALAND

Women in parliament

Percentage of seats in parliament held by women

2017 or latest available data

- more than 30%
- 21% – 30%
- 11% – 20%
- 10% or fewer
- no data

Included: all heads of government and acting heads of government in power for 100 days or more.

Excluded: heads of state and acting heads of government in power for fewer than 100 days.
2018

In the 1950s, women as heads of democratic governments were unknown; in the 1960s and 1970s, they were a rarity; in the 1980s and 1990s they were uncommon but getting steadily less so. Yet today the question remains, why so few? Only 60 democratic countries have ever had a woman head of government, even counting appointed prime ministers in presidential systems.

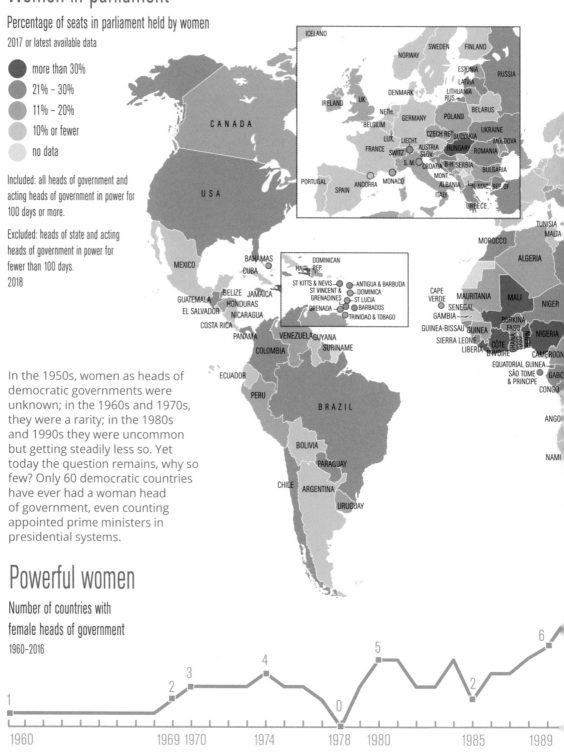

Powerful women

Number of countries with female heads of government

1960–2016

RUSSIA

KAZAKHSTAN

MONGOLIA

GEORGIA
TURKEY ARMENIA AZER.
UZBEKISTAN KYRGYZSTAN

NORTH
KOREA JAPAN

TURKMEN.
TAJIKISTAN

SOUTH
KOREA

CYPRUS SYRIA LEB.
ISRAEL
PALESTINE JORDAN IRAQ
IRAN AFGHANISTAN

CHINA

BAHRAIN KUWAIT
QATAR
U.A.E.
PAKISTAN

NEPAL BHUTAN

EGYPT SAUDI
ARABIA OMAN

INDIA BANGLADESH
LAOS

MYANMAR

PHILIPPINES

SUDAN ERITREA YEMEN

THAILAND VIETNAM

DJIBOUTI

CAMBODIA

C.A.R. SOUTH
SUDAN ETHIOPIA

SRI LANKA

BRUNEI

D.R. CONGO UGANDA SOMALIA

MALDIVES

MALAYSIA

SINGAPORE

RWANDA KENYA
BURUNDI

SEYCHELLES

INDONESIA

PAPUA
NEW
GUINEA

SOLOMON
ISLANDS

TANZANIA

COMOROS

TIMOR-LESTE

ZAMBIA MALAWI

MADAGASCAR

MAURITIUS

ZIMBABWE

AUSTRALIA

BOTSWANA MOZAMBIQUE

SWAZILAND

SOUTH LESOTHO
AFRICA

NEW
ZEALAND

MICRONESIA, FED. ST. OF
MARSHALL ISLANDS
PALAU
NAURU
KIRIBATI
TUVALU

SAMOA

VANUATU
FIJI

TONGA

LGBTQ+ rights

ICELAND

NORWAY SWEDEN FINLAND

ESTONIA
RUSSIA
LATVIA
LITHUANIA
DENMARK RUS.—

IRELAND
UK
NETH. POLAND BELARUS
GERMANY
BELGIUM
LUX. CZECH REP. SLOVAKIA UKRAINE
LIECHT. MOLDOVA
FRANCE AUSTRIA HUNGARY
SWITZ. SLOV. ROMANIA
S. M. CROATIA B-H SERBIA BULGARIA
PORTUGAL ANDORRA MONACO MONT.— KOSOVO
ITALY ALBANIA N. MAC., REP. OF
SPAIN
TURKEY
GREECE

CANADA

USA

MEXICO

CUBA
DOMINICAN
REP.
HAITI
ST KITTS & NEVIS — ANTIGUA & BARBUDA
BELIZE JAMAICA DOMINICA
GUATEMALA HONDURAS GRENADA ST LUCIA
EL SALVADOR NICARAGUA BARBADOS
COSTA RICA ST VINCENT & GRENADINES
TRINIDAD & TOBAGO

PANAMA
VENEZUELA
COLOMBIA GUYANA
SURINAME

ECUADOR

PERU

BRAZIL

BOLIVIA

PARAGUAY

CHILE ARGENTINA

URUGUAY

TUNISIA
MALTA
MOROCCO
ALGERIA LIBYA

CAPE MAURITANIA MALI NIGER
VERDE CHAD
SENEGAL
GAMBIA BURKINA
GUINEA-BISSAU GUINEA FASO Northern Nigeria
CÔTE BENIN
SIERRA LEONE D'IVOIRE GHANA NIGERIA C.A.R.
LIBERIA TOGO CAMEROON
EQUATORIAL
GUINEA — GABON D.R
SÃO TOME CONG
& PRINCIPE CONGO

ANGOLA

NAMIBIA

BOTSWA

SOU
AFR

In 127 countries
and territories,
sexual activity and
relationships between
people of the same sex
are permitted by law. In
69 countries, they are illegal.
The reality experienced by
LGBTQ+ people is much more
diverse than that implies. There
remain many countries where
same-sex relations are legal for
women but not men, many where
social reality is more oppressive
than the law, and others where it
is more liberal. The extent of legal
rights varies considerably, even in
countries where homosexuality
is legal – just as the degree of
punishment varies where it is illegal.

Legal status

Of same-sex sexual acts & relationships

2019

Punishment where illegal:

- death penalty
- prison sentence over 10 years
- prison sentence up to 10 years

Extent of right where legal:

- same-sex acts legal but no legal status for same-sex relationships
- civil partnership/union allowed
- full marriage rights for same-sex couples
- legal status unclear
- no data

The right to adopt

joint adoption by same-sex couples allowed

Acceptance of LGB people in military

2019

Lesbian, gay, and bisexual people:

- may serve in the military
- may not serve in the military
- no data

CANADA

USA

CUBA

BELIZE

JAMAICA

NICARAGUA

COLOMBIA

ECUADOR

PERU

BRAZIL

BOLIVIA

CHILE

ARGENTINA

URUGUAY

NORWAY

SWEDEN

FINLAND

ESTONIA

LATVIA

LITHUANIA

RUS.

RUSSIA

DENMARK

BELARUS

IRELAND

UK

NETH.

GERMANY

POLAND

UKRAINE

BELGIUM

LUX.

CZECH REP.

SLOVAKIA

FRANCE

SWITZ.

AUSTRIA

SLOV.

HUNGARY

ROMANIA

CROATIA

B-H

SERBIA

BULGARIA

PORTUGAL

SPAIN

ALBANIA

ITALY

GREECE

TUNISIA

MALTA

MOROCCO

ALGERIA

LIBYA

GAMBIA

SIERRA LEONE

LIBERIA

GHANA

NIGERIA

CAMEROON

NAMIBIA

The acceptability or not of LGB people serving in the military is an interesting litmus test of the degree to which acceptance of homosexuality is normalized and people are treated as citizens – with the same rights, duties, and choices – regardless of sexual preference.

Minorities

RUSSIA

RUS.

BELARUS

UKRAINE

MOLDOVA

CROATIA B-H SERBIA

KOSOVO

ALBANIA N. MAC., REP. OF

TUNISIA

MOROCCO

ALGERIA

LIBYA

MEXICO

CUBA

DOMINICAN
REP.

JAMAICA

HAITI

MAURITANIA MALI

NIGER

CHAD

GUATEMALA

EL SALVADOR HONDURAS

NICARAGUA

SENEGAL

GAMBIA

GUINEA-BISSAU GUINEA

SIERRA LEONE

LIBERIA

BURKINA
FASO

CÔTE
D'IVOIRE

TOGO

BENIN

NIGERIA

C.A.R.

VENEZUELA GUYANA

SURINAME

COLOMBIA

CAMEROON

EQUATORIAL GUINEA

SÃO TOME
& PRINCIPE

GABON

CONGO

D.R.
CONGO

ECUADOR

PERU

ANGOLA

BOLIVIA

PARAGUAY

ARGENTINA

The Peoples under Threat
index produced by Minorities
Rights Group International
identifies country situations
where communities face
the risk of genocide, mass
killing, or systematic violent
repression. It is based on a
range of indicators of conflict,
prior genocide or politicide,
flight, group division, and
democracy or governance
indicators, as well as the OECD
country risk classification.

Peoples under threat

Index of risk to communities
of genocide and mass killing

2019 score

20.0 or more *highest risk*

15.0 – 19.9

10.0 – 14.9

5.0 – 9.9

less than 5.0 *lowest risk*

no data or *extremely
low risk*

RUSSIA

KAZAKHSTAN

UZBEKISTAN

KYRGYZSTAN

NORTH
KOREA

GEORGIA

TURKEY

ARMENIA

AZER.

TURKMEN.

TAJIKISTAN

CHINA

SRAEL

LEB.

SYRIA

IRAQ

JORDAN

AFGHANISTAN

IRAN

PALESTINE

KUWAIT

BAHRAIN

PAKISTAN

NEPAL

BHUTAN

EGYPT

SAUDI
ARABIA

INDIA

BANGLADESH

LAOS

FIJI

SUDAN

ERITREA

YEMEN

MYANMAR

THAILAND

PHILIPPINES

DJIBOUTI

CAMBODIA

VIETNAM

SOUTH
SUDAN

ETHIOPIA

SRI LANKA

UGANDA

SOMALIA

MALDIVES

KENYA

RWANDA

BURUNDI

TANZANIA

SEYCHELLES

I N D O N E S I A

PAPUA
NEW
GUINEA

COMOROS

SOLOMON
ISLANDS

ZAMBIA

MALAWI

TIMOR-LESTE

ZIMBABWE

MOZAMBIQUE

SWAZILAND

Freedom

Freedom House classifies
countries and territories
according to the political rights
and civil liberties enjoyed by
individuals, using information
from 25 indicators, based on
the principles expressed in the
Universal Declaration of
Human Rights.

Freedom in the world

Freedom House rating
2018

● free   ● partly free   ● not free

○ disputed territories

South Ossetia

Pakistani Kashmir

Nagorno-Karabakh

Indian Kashmir

RUSSIA

KAZAKHSTAN

MONGOLIA

UKRAINE

Crimea
GEORGIA

UZBEKISTAN

KYRGYZSTAN

NORTH KOREA

JAPAN

TURKEY

ARMENIA

AZER.

TURKMEN.

TAJIKISTAN

SOUTH KOREA

N. CYPRUS (Turk.)

CYPRUS
LEB.
ISRAEL

SYRIA

IRAQ

IRAN

AFGHANISTAN

CHINA

PALESTINE

JORDAN

KUWAIT

BAHRAIN

PAKISTAN

NEPAL

BHUTAN

EGYPT

QATAR
U.A.E

SAUDI ARABIA

OMAN

INDIA

BANGLADESH

LAOS

TAIWAN

HONG KONG SAR (CHINA)

SUDAN

ERITREA

YEMEN

MYANMAR

VIETNAM

PHILIPPINES

Somaliland

CAMBODIA

SOUTH SUDAN

ETHIOPIA

DJIBOUTI

THAILAND

SRI LANKA

BRUNEI

D.R. CONGO

SOMALIA

MALDIVES

MALAYSIA

KENYA

UGANDA

SINGAPORE

RWANDA

BURUNDI

INDONESIA

PAPUA NEW GUINEA

TANZANIA

SEYCHELLES

MALAWI

COMOROS

TIMOR-LESTE

SOLOMON ISLANDS

ZAMBIA

MADAGASCAR

MAURITIUS

ZIMBABWE

MOZAMBIQUE

AUSTRALIA

SWAZILAND

LESOTHO

MICRONESIA, FED. ST. OF

MARSHALL ISLANDS

PALAU

NAURU

KIRIBATI

TUVALU

SAMOA

VANUATU

FIJI

TONGA

NEW ZEALAND

Changing times

Increase or decrease in freedom

2008–2018

↑ increase

↓ decrease

War and peace

Any war is too much war. That said, from 1995 to 2010 there were fewer, less lethal wars each year. This was the peace dividend from the end of the Cold War in 1990, along with a reduced risk of nuclear conflagration and the use of more economic resources for peaceful purposes. It was possible because international cooperation increased and helped end wars and monitor peace agreements.

But those gains have not been sustained. Since 2010, the number of wars has increased, the number of international peace operations has declined, the number of new peace agreements has fallen away, and the rate of casualties from war has risen sharply.

Military spending also picked up pace in 1999, increasing every year until 2012, when it stabilised following the 2008 to 2009 financial and economic crisis, before starting to increase again in 2015. The global total is now as high as just before the end of the Cold War. Whether the economic impact of the Covid-19 pandemic will slow spending again has yet to be seen.

There are still around 13,000 nuclear warheads in the world. Even a handful striking a country would be a disaster so these arsenals are hardly insignificant, but compared to 65,000 or so warheads at the height of the Cold War, the reduction has been a real achievement. Unfortunately, it is unclear how strong the commitment is to further reductions. The USA and Russia each claimed the other cheated over the Intermediate Nuclear Forces Treaty of 1987; the USA announced it would abandon the treaty in 2018 and Russia followed suit. During 2019 and 2020, neither country would commit to continuing a treaty that limits long-range missiles and bombers.

All this reflects the increasingly toxic nature of geopolitics, both at the global level – USA vs China, NATO vs Russia – and in regional rivalries such as between Iran and Saudi Arabia, and India and Pakistan. That toxin hinders cooperation to end armed conflicts. It is the reason why the global system of conflict management is weaker than at any time since 1990. And it means that the appetite for cooperation is declining at the very moment when the world faces a range of challenges – climate change, pandemics, potential cyber vulnerability – to which responding cooperatively is the realistic way forward.

Wars this century

At war

Presence of open armed conflict for political goals
2000–2019

has experienced armed conflict within national borders

armed conflict active within national borders as of 2 November 2019

has *also* sent 500 or more troops to fight in war outside national borders

has *only* fought war outside national borders

has not experienced armed conflict

RUSSIA

KAZAKHSTAN

MONGOLIA

ARUS

KRAINE

MOLDOVA

GEORGIA

UZBEKISTAN

KYRGYZSTAN

NORTH KOREA

JAPAN

MICRONESIA, FED. ST. OF

MARSHALL ISLANDS

ARMENIA

AZER.

TURKMEN.

TAJIKISTAN

SOUTH KOREA

TURKEY

CYPRUS (Turk.)

LEB.

SYRIA

AFGHANISTAN

CHINA

KIRIBATI

CYPRUS

ISRAEL

IRAQ

IRAN

JORDAN

PALESTINE

KUWAIT

PAKISTAN

NEPAL

BHUTAN

TAIWAN

EGYPT

BAHRAIN

QATAR

U.A.E.

BANGLADESH

SAMOA

SAUDI ARABIA

INDIA

MYANMAR

LAOS

SUDAN

OMAN

YEMEN

THAILAND

VIETNAM

PHILIPPINES

FIJI

ERITREA

DJIBOUTI

SOMALILAND

CAMBODIA

SOUTH SUDAN

ETHIOPIA

PUNTLAND

SRI LANKA

BRUNEI

TONGA

UGANDA

SOMALIA

MALDIVES

MALAYSIA

KENYA

SINGAPORE

RWANDA

BURUNDI

SEYCHELLES

PAPUA NEW GUINEA

TANZANIA

SOLOMON ISLANDS

INDONESIA

COMOROS

TIMOR-LESTE

ZAMBIA

MALAWI

MADAGASCAR

MAURITIUS

ZIMBABWE

TSWANA

MOZAMBIQUE

AUSTRALIA

UTH RICA

SWAZILAND

LESOTHO

For 20 years after the US–Soviet Cold War ended in 1990, the world experienced a peace dividend. Though warfare continued, often on a horrifying scale – Rwanda in 1994, Bosnia and Herzegovina in 1992–95, Sudan until 2011, Iraq in 1991 and again from 2003 on – there were actually fewer wars and fewer fatalities. Compared to 50 armed conflicts in 1990, by 2010 there were 31. But then the number increased again, to 52 by 2019.

NEW ZEALAND

Fighting outside borders

Afghanistan

Countries involved at some point since 2001

as of 2018

- location of war
- NATO members
- other participating countries

NATO members: Albania, Belgium, Bulgaria, Canada, Croatia, Czech Republic, Denmark, Estonia, France, Germany, Greece, Hungary, Iceland, Italy, Latvia, Lithuania, Luxembourg, Montenegro, Netherlands, Norway, Poland, Portugal, Romania, Slovakia, Slovenia, Spain, Turkey, UK, USA

Other participants: Armenia, Australia, Austria, Azerbaijan, Bahrain, Bosnia-Herzegovina, El Salvador, Finland, Georgia, Iran, Ireland, Jordan, North Macedonia, Malaysia, Mongolia, New Zealand, Pakistan, Singapore, South Korea, Sweden, Switzerland, Tonga, Ukraine, United Arab Emirates

Iraq

Countries involved at some point since 2003

as of end 2018

- location of war
- participating countries

Albania, Armenia, Australia, Azerbaijan, Bahrain, Belgium, Bosnia-Herzegovina, Bulgaria, Canada, Czech Republic, Denmark, Estonia, France, Georgia, Honduras, Italy, Jordan, Kazakhstan, Latvia, Lithuania, North Macedonia, Moldova, Mongolia, Netherlands, Nicaragua, Norway, Philippines, Poland, Portugal, Romania, Saudi Arabia, Slovakia, South Korea, Spain, Tonga, Ukraine, UAE, UK, USA

D.R. Congo

Countries involved in 2000, 2013, 2017

- location of war
- participating countries

Angola, Burundi, Chad, Namibia, Rwanda, Sudan, Uganda, Zimbabwe

Somalia

Countries involved at some point since 2007

- location of war
- participating countries

Burundi, Djibouti, Ethiopia, Ghana, Kenya, Nigeria, Sierra Leone, Uganda, USA

Yemen

Countries involved at some point since 2011
as of end 2018

- location of war
- participating countries

Bahrain, Egypt, Jordan, Kuwait, Morocco, Qatar, Saudi Arabia, Sudan, UAE, USA

Warlords, ganglords, and militias

Non-state armed forces

Estimated strength of non-state armed forces in all countries

latest available data 2010–2019

10,000 or more

fewer than 10,000

unknown strength

no known non-state armed force

armed conflict fought between non-state forces

Non-state wars

Armed conflicts do not only occur within or between states. The number of armed conflicts in which no state has any part is now greater than the number of armed conflicts involving states – 80 without states in 2019 compared to 52 with states.

Along with that, there has been a marked proliferation of non-state armed forces. By one estimate, the number of armed groups active per armed conflict was 8 in 1950, increasing to 14 in 2010. But even that figure is modest by current standards: in warfare in Syria since 2011, over 1,000 separate armed groups have been identified – in Libya in the same period some 2,000.

The power of private armies and the risk of non-state wars grow when and where the state's ability to impose order is weak. In some parts of some countries the state is essentially absent for extended periods, sometimes because of war, sometimes corruption, and sometimes because the state simply cannot afford to obtain the equipment and train the forces it would need in order to control its territory.

Many militias continue to operate long after the war is over. In those circumstances, local leaders emerge, often enriching themselves by controlling key economic activities: small-scale mining, as in eastern DRC, or the narcotics trade, as in Colombia, Mexico, and Central Asia. If the state does try to restore its authority, its soldiers all too often become part of the problem, terrorizing civilians with theft, rape, and other human rights abuses.

One common abuse in which militias lead the way is recruiting children to fight, often forcibly, always with a brutal, traumatizing impact on the children's lives – even if they survive the war.

Colombia

Colombia
293 children used

Children at war

Used by non-state armed forces as verified by the UN

2018

Mali — 114 children used as combatants

Iraq — ISIL used a boy to drive a car bomb

Lebanon
Palestine Syria Afghanistan
Libya Iraq
Mali Pakistan
Sudan Yemen India Myanmar
Nigeria S.Sudan
C.A.R. Somalia
D.R. Congo
Philippines

Afghanistan — 46 children used for combat, to plant IEDs, to carry out suicide attacks, for sexual exploitation

Somalia — 2,300 children used

Yemen — 370 children used, more than a third as combatants

Syria — 670 boys and 136 girls used mostly as combatants

Central African Republic — 75 children used as combatants, informants, porters, cooks, servants, and for sexual purposes

Nigeria — 1,596 boys and 351 girls used, some for bearing and detonating improvised explosive devices

Philippines — 19 children used as human shields, to extract gunpowder from firecrackers, or to ransack houses

Military muscle

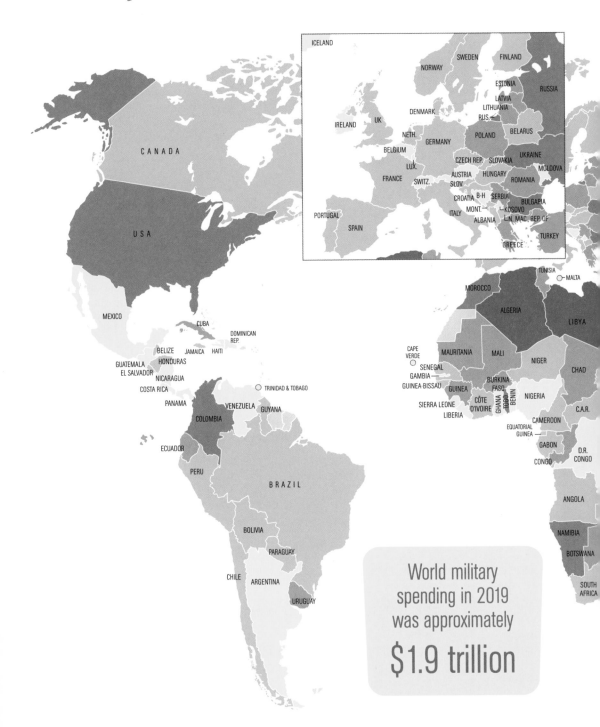

ICELAND
NORWAY
SWEDEN
FINLAND
ESTONIA
LATVIA
LITHUANIA
RUSSIA
RUS.
DENMARK
IRELAND
UK
NETH.
GERMANY
POLAND
BELARUS
BELGIUM
LUX.
CZECH REP.
SLOVAKIA
UKRAINE
FRANCE
SWITZ.
AUSTRIA
HUNGARY
MOLDOVA
SLOV.
ROMANIA
CROATIA
B-H
SERBIA
BULGARIA
PORTUGAL
MONT.
KOSOVO
SPAIN
ITALY
ALBANIA
N. MAC.
REP. OF
GREECE
TURKEY

CANADA

USA

MEXICO

BELIZE
JAMAICA
HAITI
GUATEMALA
HONDURAS
EL SALVADOR
NICARAGUA
COSTA RICA
PANAMA

CUBA
DOMINICAN
REP.

TRINIDAD & TOBAGO

VENEZUELA
GUYANA
COLOMBIA
ECUADOR

PERU

BRAZIL

BOLIVIA

PARAGUAY

CHILE
ARGENTINA

URUGUAY

TUNISIA
MALTA
MOROCCO
ALGERIA
LIBYA

CAPE
VERDE
MAURITANIA
MALI
NIGER
CHAD
SENEGAL
GAMBIA
BURKINA
GUINEA-BISSAU
GUINEA
FASO
NIGERIA
SIERRA LEONE
CÔTE
GHANA
BENIN
TOGO
LIBERIA
D'IVOIRE
CAMEROON
C.A.R.
EQUATORIAL
GUINEA
GABON
D.R.
CONGO
CONGO

ANGOLA

NAMIBIA
BOTSWANA

SOUTH
AFRICA

World military
spending in 2019
was approximately

$1.9 trillion

Military spending

Military expenditure as a percentage of GDP

2019 or latest available data

- 4.0% or more
- 3.0% – 3.9%
- 2.0% – 2.9%
- 1.0% – 1.9%
- less than 1.0%
- no data

Top military spenders

US$ at 2018 constant prices

 2001 ● 2009 ● 2019

At just under $2 trillion, world military spending in 2019 was the highest since 1988, but levels of spending have fluctuated over the years. The annual total fell from

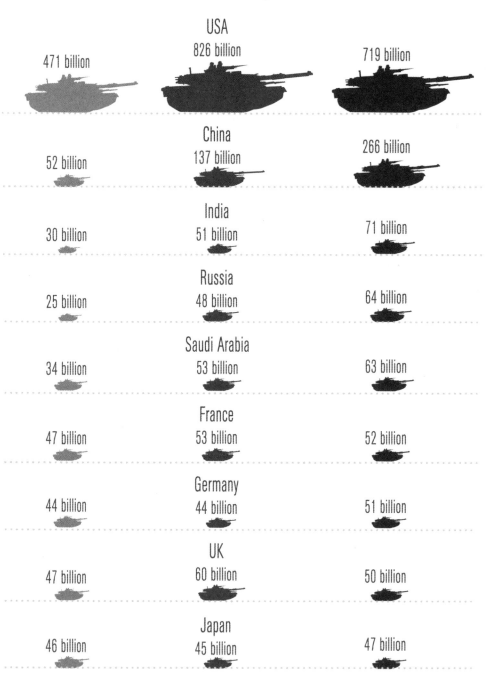

USA
471 billion
826 billion
719 billion

China
52 billion
137 billion
266 billion

India
30 billion
51 billion
71 billion

Russia
25 billion
48 billion
64 billion

Saudi Arabia
34 billion
53 billion
63 billion

France
47 billion
53 billion
52 billion

Germany
44 billion
44 billion
51 billion

UK
47 billion
60 billion
50 billion

Japan
46 billion
45 billion
47 billion

2011 through 2014 in the wake of the 2008–09 global economic and financial crisis. From 2015, military spending increased steadily. The economic impact of the Covid-19 pandemic means 2019 might turn out to have been a peak year.

Levels of military spending – as of all government spending – reflect priorities and choices about where to use resources. More military spending does not automatically mean more military power, let alone more real security.

Armed forces top ten

Largest regular armed forces

2020

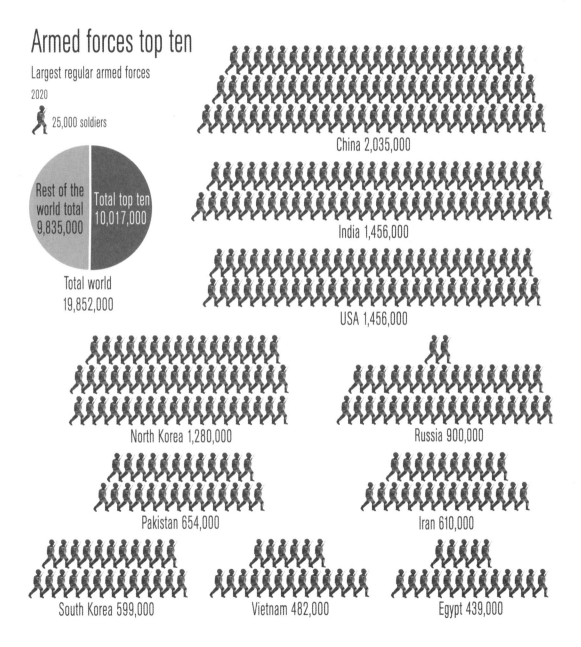

25,000 soldiers

Rest of the world total 9,835,000

Total top ten 10,017,000

Total world 19,852,000

China 2,035,000

India 1,456,000

USA 1,456,000

North Korea 1,280,000

Russia 900,000

Pakistan 654,000

Iran 610,000

South Korea 599,000

Vietnam 482,000

Egypt 439,000

Mass destruction

Declining stockpiles of nuclear warheads

1985–2019

In 2019, the global nuclear stockpile amounted to 13,850 warheads and bombs. This was dramatically fewer than the 65,000 to 70,000 bombs and warheads stockpiled in the mid-1980s at the height of the Cold War. Two-thirds of each of the US and Russian stockpiles today are inactive – either in storage or waiting to be dismantled.

━━ USA   ━━ USSR

45,000

39,197

37,000

27,000

21,000

17,000

12,000

7,500

6,500

24,237

21,004

12,144

10,577

10,295

9,600

7,260

6,185

1985 1986   1990   1995   2000   2005   2010   2015   2019

Nuclear accidents

Officially or unofficially reported incident

1950–2000

Responsibility of UK

Responsibility of USA

Responsibility of USSR

Many accidents with nuclear weapons and waste have been recorded, including: accidental or unauthorized firing; nuclear detonation; non-nuclear detonation or burning of a nuclear weapon or radioactive component; radioactive contamination; theft, accidental jettisoning; public hazard; false alerts of incoming nuclear attack.

YEAR	LOCATION
1950	British Columbia, Canada
	New Mexico, USA
	Ohio, USA
	California, USA
	Quebec, Canada
	Alaska, USA
	Mediterranean Sea
1952	UK
1956	New Mexico, USA
1957	New Mexico, USA
	Florida, USA
	Atlantic Ocean
	Florida, USA
1958	overseas base
	off Georgia coast, USA
	Greenham Common, UK
	off Georgia coast, USA
	Georgia, USA
	Texas, USA
	Louisiana, USA
	South Carolina, USA
	Urals, USSR
1959	unspecified Pacific base
	Louisiana, USA
	Washington, USA
	Kentucky, USA
	Florida, USA
1960	New Jersey, USA
1961	Utah, USA
	North Carolina, USA
	California, USA
	North Sea
1962	US Pacific Test Range

Nuclear warhead stockpiles

2019

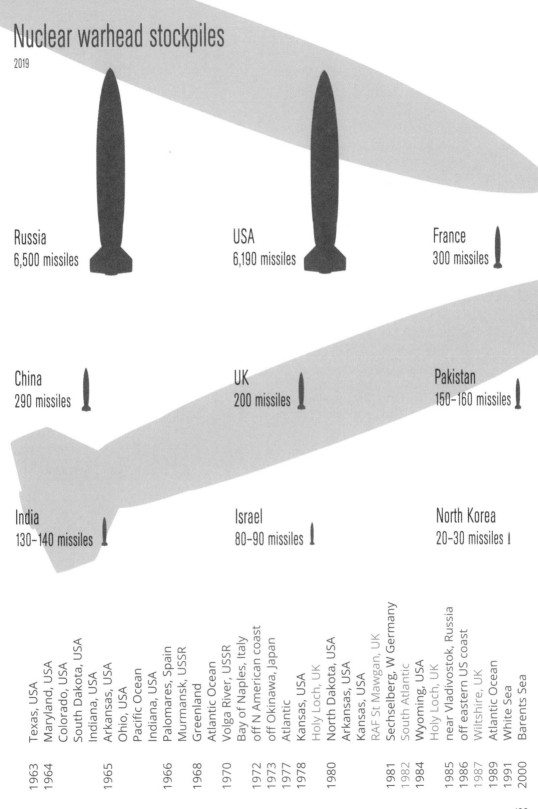

Russia
6,500 missiles

USA
6,190 missiles

France
300 missiles

China
290 missiles

UK
200 missiles

Pakistan
150–160 missiles

India
130–140 missiles

Israel
80–90 missiles

North Korea
20–30 missiles

1963	Texas, USA
1964	Maryland, USA
	Colorado, USA
	South Dakota, USA
	Indiana, USA
1965	Arkansas, USA
	Ohio, USA
	Pacific Ocean
	Indiana, USA
1966	Palomares, Spain
	Murmansk, USSR
	Greenland
1968	Atlantic Ocean
1970	Volga River, USSR
	Bay of Naples, Italy
1972	off N American coast
1973	off Okinawa, Japan
1977	Atlantic
1978	Kansas, USA
	Holy Loch, UK
1980	North Dakota, USA
	Arkansas, USA
	Kansas, USA
	RAF St Mawgan, UK
1981	Sechselberg, W Germany
1982	South Atlantic
1984	Wyoming, USA
	Holy Loch, UK
1985	near Vladivostok, Russia
1986	off eastern US coast
1987	Wiltshire, UK
1989	Atlantic Ocean
1991	White Sea
2000	Barents Sea

Chemical weapons in Syria

2012   July: Syrian Foreign Ministry confirms that Syria has chemical weapons.

2012   Dec: Allegation of use of chemical weapons in Syria.

2013   Mar: Allegation of use of chemical weapons. UN announces investigation in collaboration with WHO and OPCW.

2013   Apr: Two allegations of use of chemical weapons.

2013   Aug: Allegation of use of chemical weapons. UN investigators attacked by snipers in Syria.

2013   Sept: USA & Russia agree plan for accounting, inspection, control, and elimination of Syria's chemical weapons. Syria submits declaration of stockpiles of chemical weapons to the OPCW.

2013   Oct: Destruction of Syria's stockpiles of chemical weapons begins. All declared facilities for mixing and producing chemical weapons are destroyed, or rendered inoperable.

2013   Nov: OPCW approves plan for removal of Syria's chemical weapons by ship from country.

2014   Jan–April: 80% of chemical weapons and 92% of chemical agents removed.

2014   April: Allegation of use of chemical weapons.

2014   June: OPCW confirms use of chlorine gas in earlier attacks.

2014   June: OPCW announces removal of all chemical weapons from Syria.

2014   Sept: OPCW confirms use of chlorine gas.

2015   Mar: UN Security Council adopts resolution condemning use of chlorine as a weapon in Syria's civil war and threatening action under Chapter VII of the UN Charter if action repeated.

2015   Apr: Allegation of use of chemical weapons.

Use of chemical agents in warfare has been rare since World War I, when they caused 1.3 million casualties, including 90,000 deaths. They were allegedly used in Yemen by Egyptian forces in the 1960s and were used by Iraq against Iranian forces and Kurdish civilians in the 1980s. They were used in terrorism in Japan in the 1990s and for political assassinations in the UK in 2006 and 2018, and in Malaysia in 2017. And they have been used in Syria since 2012. Their production, stockpiling, and use is outlawed by the Chemical Weapons Convention of 1997.

SYRIA

1 ○
Al-Hasakah

1 ●
2 ●●
○
Deir Ezzor

Chemical attacks in Syria

Number of incidents in each governate of Syria
as of 23 January 2019

Perpetrator: Assad regime, except for releases of
mustard gas by ISIS in Aleppo and Al-Hasakah

○ incident comprehensively confirmed
investigated and confirmed by competent international
bodies or backed up by at least three highly reliable
independent sources

○ incident confirmed
backed up by at least two highly reliable sources or
three or more independent secondary sources

● chlorine

● sarin

○ mustard gas/sulfur mustard

○ unknown

2016	Aug: Allegation of use of chemical weapons.
2016	Aug: OPCW finds Syrian government responsible for chemical weapons attacks in April 2014 & March 2015, Islamic State responsible for use of sulfur mustard in August 2015.
2016	Sept: Allegation of use of chemical weapons.
2016	Oct: OPCW finds Syrian regime responsible for chlorine gas use in March 2015
2016	Dec: Allegation of use of chemical weapons.
2017	Apr: Allegation of use of chemical weapons. USA uses Tomahawk cruise missiles to attack Syrian airbase from which it believes chemical weapons attack was launched.
2017	Apr: OPCW confirms that sarin was used.
2017	June: OPCW finds Syrian regime responsible for April 2017 attack, and Islamic State responsible for use of sulfur mustard in Sept 2016.
2018	Feb: Allegation of use of chemical weapons.
2018	Apr: Allegation of use of chemical weapons.
2018	May: OPCW finds it likely that chemical weapons were used in February 2018.
2018	June: OPCW finds it very likely that sarin was used twice in March 2017.
2018	Sept: Independent International Commission of Inquiry on the Syrian Arab Republic, appointed by UN, finds that Syrian government used chlorine as a weapon four times from Jan–July 2018.
2019	Mar: OPCW reports that chemical weapons were used in April 2018.

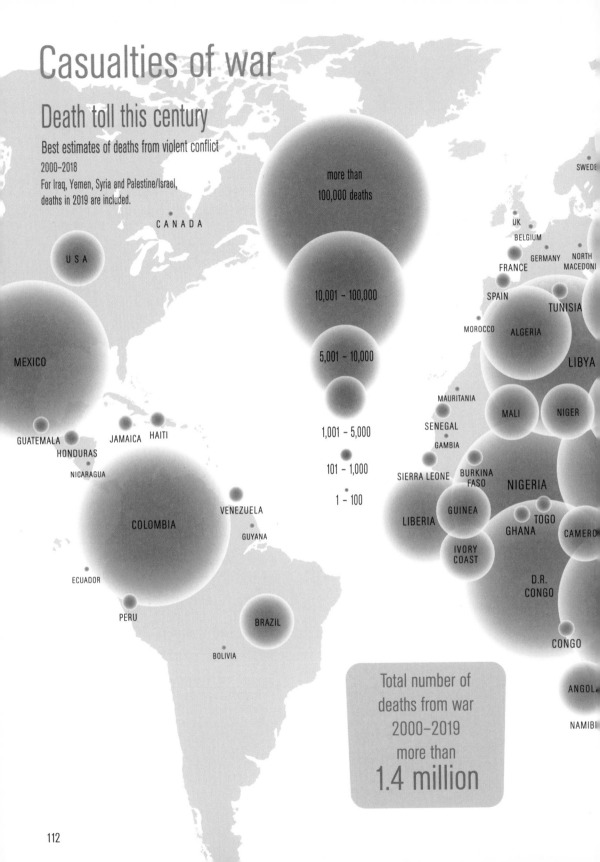

Casualties of war

Death toll this century

Best estimates of deaths from violent conflict

2000–2018
For Iraq, Yemen, Syria and Palestine/Israel,
deaths in 2019 are included.

more than
100,000 deaths

10,001 – 100,000

5,001 – 10,000

1,001 – 5,000

101 – 1,000

1 – 100

CANADA

USA

MEXICO

GUATEMALA
HONDURAS
NICARAGUA

JAMAICA   HAITI

VENEZUELA

GUYANA

COLOMBIA

ECUADOR

PERU

BRAZIL

BOLIVIA

SWEDE

UK
BELGIUM
GERMANY   NORTH
MACEDONI
FRANCE
SPAIN
TUNISIA

MOROCCO   ALGERIA

LIBYA

MAURITANIA
SENEGAL
GAMBIA

MALI   NIGER

SIERRA LEONE   BURKINA
FASO
NIGERIA

LIBERIA   GUINEA
TOGO
GHANA   CAMERO

IVORY
COAST

D.R.
CONGO

CONGO

ANGOLA

NAMIBI

Total number of
deaths from war
2000–2019
more than
1.4 million

UKRAINE

RUSSIA

AFGHANISTAN

UZBEKISTAN

KYRGYZSTAN

GEORGIA

AZERBAIJAN

TAJIKISTAN

RKEY

SYRIA

ARMENIA

CHINA

LEBANON

IRAQ

AEL &
ESTINE

IRAN

JORDAN

PAKISTAN

NEPAL

GYPT

SUDAN

SAUDI
ARABIA

ERITREA

KUWAIT

LAOS

HAD

BAHRAIN

UAE

DJIBOUTI

YEMEN

THAILAND

BANGLADESH

CAMBODIA

PHILIPPINES

OUTH
UDAN

ETHIOPIA

INDIA

MYANMAR

MALAYSIA

UGANDA

KENYA

ENTRAL
FRICAN
PUBLIC

RWANDA

SOMALIA

PAPUA
NEW GUINEA

TANZANIA

BURUNDI

SRI LANKA

INDONESIA

MADAGASCAR

ZAMBIA

MOZAMBIQUE

AUSTRALIA

ZIMBABWE

UTH
RICA

Increasing death toll

Reliable statistics on deaths in war do not exist. There are several reasons why. The figures are manipulated up or down for competing propaganda purposes. In many wars the dangers and complexities of compiling reliable data are simply too great. Though the number of people who die in battle, whether they are fighters or civilians, can sometimes be counted or well estimated, it is often impossible to know anything about the numbers who die through indirect effects – such as from the spread of disease because water systems are destroyed, or from injuries or illnesses that cannot be medically treated because hospitals are destroyed.

Regional toll

Best estimates of combat deaths in armed conflict

10,000 deaths 2000–2010
10,000 deaths 2011–2018/19

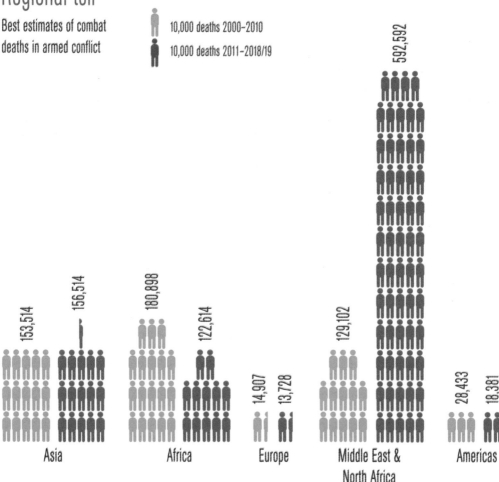

Asia	Africa	Europe	Middle East & North Africa	Americas
153,514 156,514	180,898 122,614	14,907 13,728	129,102 592,592	28,433 18,381

Estimates are nonetheless available. Of varying reliability in detail, the big picture trends they show tend to be more dependable. The Middle East and North Africa has been a crucible of war and violence this century. The biggest element of the region's death toll in the first decade (2000–2010) was the war in Iraq, starting with the US-led invasion in 2003. The biggest element in the second decade has been warfare in Syria. Meanwhile, in Africa, though armed conflict persists in many countries, the toll has reduced by about one-third from the century's first to second decades.

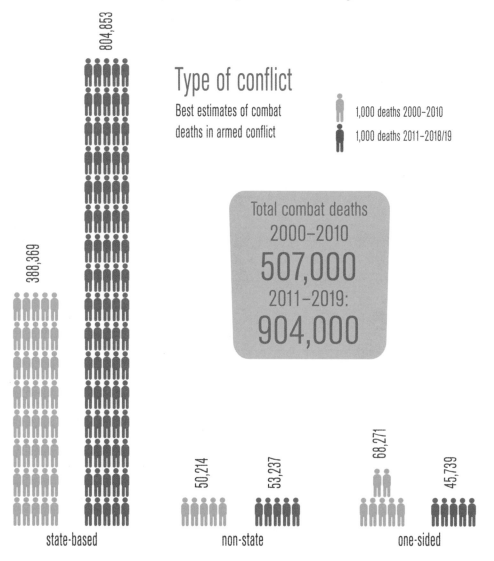

Type of conflict

Best estimates of combat deaths in armed conflict

1,000 deaths 2000–2010
1,000 deaths 2011–2018/19

Total combat deaths
2000–2010
507,000
2011–2019:
904,000

804,853
388,369
state-based

50,214
53,237
non-state

68,271
45,739
one-sided

Terrorism

ICELAND

GREENLAND (Den)

NORWAY
SWEDEN
FINLAND
ESTONIA
RUSSIA
LATVIA
LITHUANIA
DENMARK
RUS.
IRELAND
UK
NETH.
GERMANY
POLAND
BELARUS
BELGIUM
CZECH REP.
SLOVAKIA
UKRAINE
MOLDOVA
FRANCE
SWITZ.
AUSTRIA
HUNGARY
ROMANIA
SLOV.
CROATIA
B-H
SERBIA
BULGARIA
ITALY
MONT.
KOSOVO
PORTUGAL
ALBANIA
N. MAC.
REP. OF
SPAIN
TURKEY
GREECE

CANADA

USA

MEXICO

BAHAMAS
CUBA
DOMINICAN
REP.
BELIZE
JAMAICA
HAITI
GUATEMALA
HONDURAS
EL SALVADOR
NICARAGUA
GRENADA
COSTA RICA
TRINIDAD & TOBAGO
PANAMA
VENEZUELA
GUYANA
COLOMBIA
SURINAME

ECUADOR

PERU

BRAZIL

BOLIVIA

PARAGUAY

CHILE
ARGENTINA

URUGUAY

TUNISIA
MALTA
MOROCCO
ALGERIA
LIBYA
WESTERN
SAHARA (Mor.)
MAURITANIA
MALI
NIGER
CHAD
SENEGAL
GAMBIA
BURKINA
GUINEA-BISSAU
GUINEA
FASO
NIGERIA
SIERRA LEONE
CÔTE
GHANA
TOGO
BENIN
D'IVOIRE
LIBERIA
CAMEROON
EQUATORIAL
GUINEA
GABON
D.R.
CONGO
CONGO

ANGOLA

NAMIBIA

BOTSWA

SO
AF

In 2009–2018
there were

84,000

terrorist incidents:
21% armed assaults;
52% bombings

Incidents

Number of intentional violent
attacks by non-state actors
2009–2018

- more than 10,000
- 1,001 – 10,000
- 501 – 1,000
- 101 – 500
- 1 – 100
- no incident

RUSSIA

KAZAKHSTAN

MONGOLIA

GUAM (USA)

UZBEKISTAN

KYRGYZSTAN

NORTH KOREA

JAPAN

GEORGIA

ARMENIA AZER. TURKMEN.

TAJIKISTAN

SOUTH KOREA

CYPRUS (Turk)

PRUS LEB.

SYRIA

ISRAEL

IRAQ

IRAN

AFGHANISTAN

CHINA

PALESTINE

JORDAN

KUWAIT

PAKISTAN

NEPAL BHUTAN

TAIWAN

BAHRAIN

QATAR

U.A.E.

HONG KONG SAR (CHINA)

EGYPT

SAUDI ARABIA

OMAN

INDIA

BANGLADESH

MYANMAR

LAOS

PHILIPPINES

FIJI

SUDAN

ERITREA YEMEN

THAILAND

VIETNAM

DJIBOUTI

CAMBODIA

NEW CALEDONIA (Fr)

SOUTH SUDAN

ETHIOPIA

SRI LANKA

BRUNEI

UGANDA

SOMALIA

MALDIVES

MALAYSIA

SINGAPORE

KENYA

RWANDA

BURUNDI

TANZANIA

COMOROS

INDONESIA

PAPUA NEW GUINEA

AMBIA MALAWI

MADAGASCAR

TIMOR-LESTE

IMBABWE

MOZAMBIQUE

SWAZILAND

AUSTRALIA

LESOTHO

Of 84,000
terrorist incidents
2009–2018, almost

50%

took place in just
three countries

NEW ZEALAND

Refugees

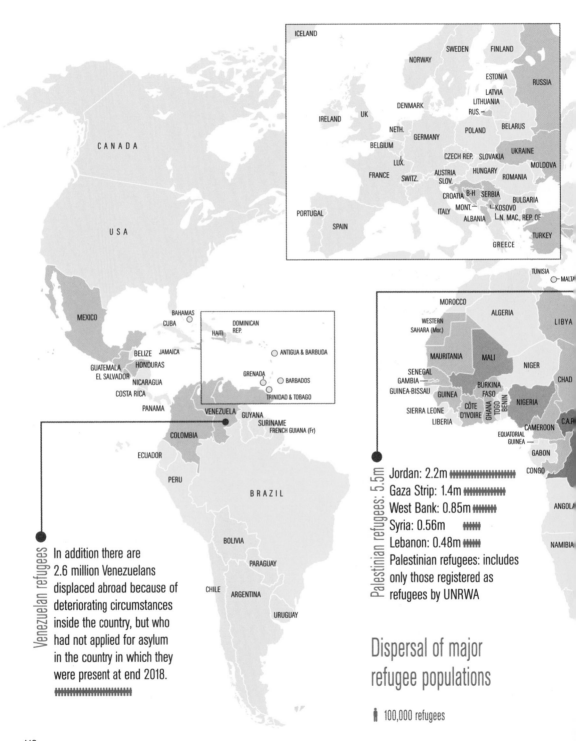

ICELAND
NORWAY SWEDEN FINLAND
ESTONIA
LATVIA RUSSIA
DENMARK LITHUANIA
IRELAND UK RUS.
NETH. POLAND BELARUS
BELGIUM GERMANY
LUX. CZECH REP. SLOVAKIA UKRAINE
FRANCE SWITZ. AUSTRIA HUNGARY MOLDOVA
SLOV. ROMANIA
CROATIA B-H SERBIA BULGARIA
PORTUGAL ITALY MONT. KOSOVO
SPAIN ALBANIA N. MAC. REP. OF
GREECE TURKEY

CANADA

USA

MEXICO
BAHAMAS
CUBA
HAITI DOMINICAN REP.
BELIZE JAMAICA
GUATEMALA HONDURAS
EL SALVADOR
NICARAGUA
COSTA RICA
PANAMA
VENEZUELA GUYANA
COLOMBIA SURINAME
FRENCH GUIANA (Fr)
ECUADOR

PERU
BRAZIL

BOLIVIA
PARAGUAY
CHILE ARGENTINA
URUGUAY

ANTIGUA & BARBUDA
GRENADA
BARBADOS
TRINIDAD & TOBAGO

TUNISIA MALTA
MOROCCO ALGERIA LIBYA
WESTERN SAHARA (Mor.)
MAURITANIA MALI NIGER
SENEGAL CHAD
GAMBIA BURKINA
GUINEA-BISSAU FASO NIGERIA
GUINEA CÔTE GHANA BENIN
SIERRA LEONE D'IVOIRE TOGO CAMEROON C.A.R
LIBERIA EQUATORIAL
GUINEA GABON
CONGO
ANGOLA
NAMIBIA

Venezuelan refugees

In addition there are 2.6 million Venezuelans displaced abroad because of deteriorating circumstances inside the country, but who had not applied for asylum in the country in which they were present at end 2018.

Palestinian refugees: 5.5m

Jordan: 2.2m
Gaza Strip: 1.4m
West Bank: 0.85m
Syria: 0.56m
Lebanon: 0.48m
Palestinian refugees: includes only those registered as refugees by UNRWA

Dispersal of major refugee populations

👤 100,000 refugees

118

Where refugees come from

Number of refugees by country origin

end 2018 or latest available data

1 million or more
500,000 – 999,999
100,000 – 499,999
10,000 – 99,999
1,000 – 9,999
fewer than 1,000
no data

Afghan refugees: 2.7m
Pakistan: 1.4m
Iran: 0.95m
Germany: 0.13m

Syrian refugees
Turkey: 3.6m
Lebanon: 0.94m
Jordan: 0.68m
Germany: 0.53m
Iraq: 0.25m

South Sudanese refugees: 2.3m
Sudan: 0.85m
Uganda: 0.79m
Ethiopia: 0.42m
Kenya: 0.12m

Myanmar refugees: 1.1m
Bangladesh: 0.91m
Malaysia: 0.14m

Where refugees go to

Number of refugees in country
of asylum

end 2018 or latest available data

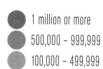

- 1 million or more
- 500,000 – 999,999
- 100,000 – 499,999
- 10,000 – 99,999
- 1,000 – 9,999
- fewer than 1,000
- no data

In 2019 there were 71 million forcibly displaced people. The number of has never been greater and it increases at an average rate of 37,000 people per day.

Many refugees are second or third generation – born in exile. Many are twice-over refugees having had to flee from the refuge to which they fled.

Internally displaced people

Number of IDPs due to conflict and violence

end 2018 or latest available data

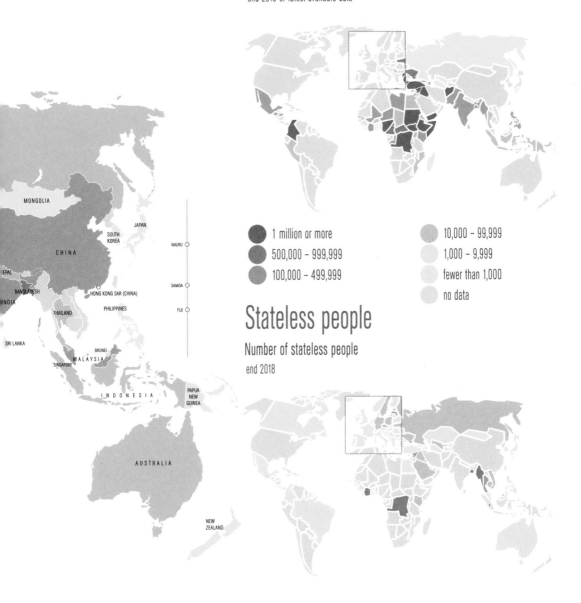

● 1 million or more

● 500,000 – 999,999

● 100,000 – 499,999

○ 10,000 – 99,999

○ 1,000 – 9,999

○ fewer than 1,000

○ no data

MONGOLIA

JAPAN

SOUTH KOREA

NAURU ○

CHINA

EPAL

SAMOA ○

BANGLADESH

HONG KONG SAR (CHINA)

NDIA

PHILIPPINES

FIJI ○

THAILAND

SRI LANKA

BRUNEI

MALAYSIA

SINGAPORE

INDONESIA

PAPUA NEW GUINEA

AUSTRALIA

NEW ZEALAND

Stateless people

Number of stateless people

end 2018

Most refugees find shelter in countries neighbouring their own. Some attempt longer, perilous journeys to seek a better future in a richer country.

Many, despite their hardships, and despite all states' legal responsibilities under the 1951 Refugee Convention, receive little or no comfort upon arrival.

Keeping the peace

Cost of violence ... and what it could be spent on

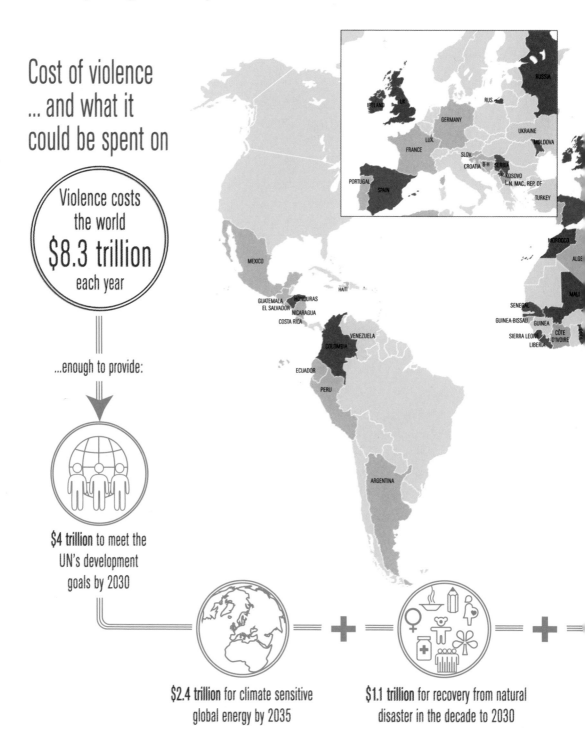

Violence costs the world **$8.3 trillion** each year

...enough to provide:

$4 trillion to meet the UN's development goals by 2030

$2.4 trillion for climate sensitive global energy by 2035

+

$1.1 trillion for recovery from natural disaster in the decade to 2030

+

Map labels:
RUSSIA, IRELAND, UK, RUS., GERMANY, UKRAINE, MOLDOVA, LUX., FRANCE, SLOV., CROATIA, B-H, SERBIA, KOSOVO, L.N. MAC., REP. OF, PORTUGAL, SPAIN, TURKEY, MOROCCO, ALGE, MALI, SENEGAL, GUINEA-BISSAU, GUINEA, SIERRA LEONE, CÔTE D'IVOIRE, LIBERIA, MEXICO, HAITI, GUATEMALA, HONDURAS, EL SALVADOR, NICARAGUA, COSTA RICA, VENEZUELA, COLOMBIA, ECUADOR, PERU, ARGENTINA

Peace agreements since 1990

Signed multiparty agreements
1990–2019

At least one agreement signed in:

- 1990s, 2000s, 2010s
- 1990s, 2000s
- 1990s, 2010s
- 2000s, 2010s
- 1990s
- 2000s
- 2010s
- no data

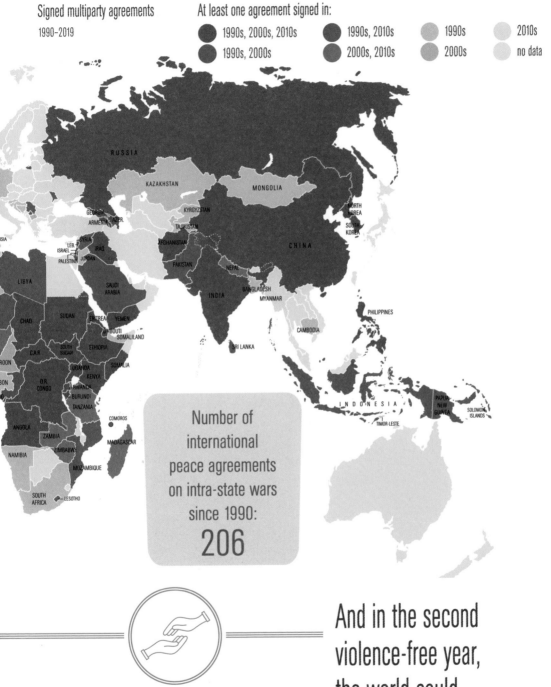

Number of
international
peace agreements
on intra-state wars
since 1990:

206

$0.2 trillion to cover costs of humanitarian assistance
needed as response to climate change by 2030

And in the second violence-free year, the world could...

Peacekeeping trends

A UN study found that in the first 12 or so years after the end of the Cold War, as many peace agreements were signed as in the previous 200 years.

The number of peace missions also increased, because the end of the confrontation between the USA and the Soviet Union freed the United Nations to do more.

UN peacekeeping missions

Number of active missions
1950–2019

Peacekeeping missions

December 2019

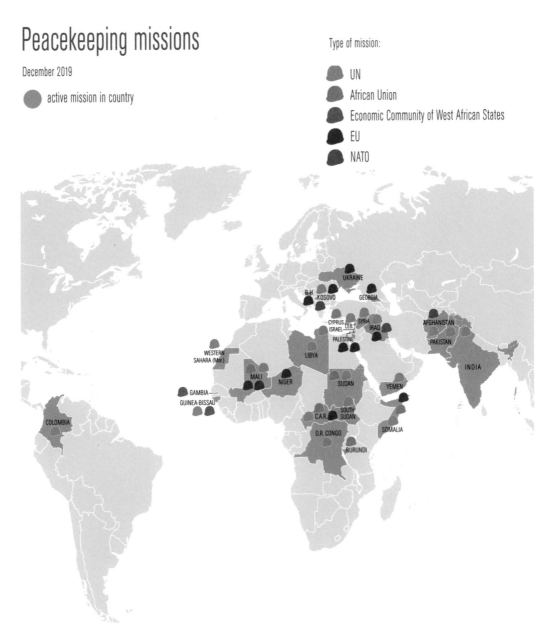

● active mission in country

Type of mission:

🪖 UN
🪖 African Union
🪖 Economic Community of West African States
🪖 EU
🪖 NATO

The number of peacekeeping missions plateaued in the mid-2000s and, although the trend is not yet clear, it looks as though it is now tailing off. This is partly an indication that several peacekeeping missions have been successfully accomplished – but may also be a sign that rich states are less willing to pay for peacekeeping in tougher economic times.

Forces for peace

Type of force
2019

 1,000 troops
 1,000 military observers
 1,000 police
 1,000 international civilian personnel

1948–2019

3,890 deaths

among UN
forces for peace

71,830 troops

Contributing to peace

Number of military and police personnel
committed to UN peacekeeping operations
October 2019

 5,000 or more
1,000 – 4,999

 500 – 999
1 – 499

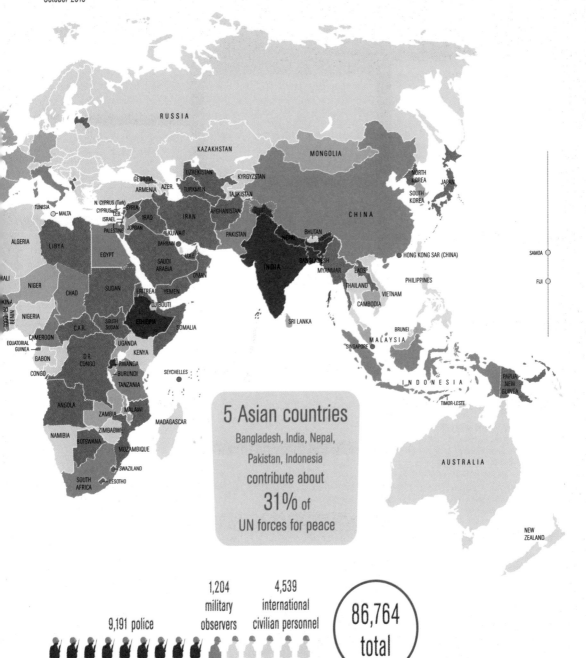

RUSSIA

KAZAKHSTAN

MONGOLIA

GEORGIA
ARMENIA AZER.
TURKMEN.
UZBEKISTAN
KYRGYZSTAN
TAJIKISTAN

NORTH
KOREA
JAPAN
SOUTH
KOREA

TUNISIA
MALTA
N. CYPRUS (Turk.)
CYPRUS
ISRAEL LEB.
PALESTINE JORDAN
SYRIA
IRAQ
IRAN
AFGHANISTAN

CHINA

HONG KONG SAR (CHINA)

SAMOA

ALGERIA
LIBYA
EGYPT
KUWAIT
BAHRAIN
SAUDI
ARABIA
U.A.E.
OMAN
PAKISTAN
NEPAL
BHUTAN
BANGLADESH
INDIA
MYANMAR
LAOS
THAILAND
VIETNAM
CAMBODIA
PHILIPPINES

FIJI

MALI
NIGER
CHAD
SUDAN
ERITREA
YEMEN
DJIBOUTI
SOMALIA
SRI LANKA

BURKINA
BENIN
TOGO
NIGERIA
C.A.R.
SOUTH
SUDAN
ETHIOPIA

BRUNEI
MALAYSIA
SINGAPORE

EQUATORIAL
GUINEA
CAMEROON
GABON
CONGO
D.R.
CONGO
UGANDA
RWANDA
BURUNDI
TANZANIA
KENYA
SEYCHELLES

INDONESIA

TIMOR-LESTE

PAPUA
NEW
GUINEA

ANGOLA
ZAMBIA
ZIMBABWE
MALAWI
MADAGASCAR

NAMIBIA
BOTSWANA
MOZAMBIQUE

AUSTRALIA

SWAZILAND
SOUTH
AFRICA
LESOTHO

5 Asian countries

Bangladesh, India, Nepal,
Pakistan, Indonesia
contribute about
31% of
UN forces for peace

NEW
ZEALAND

1,204
military
observers

4,539
international
civilian personnel

9,191 police

86,764
total

The new front line

Cyber warfare

selected incidents

Global cyber attack, 2011: The biggest reported series of cyber attacks to date hit 72 organizations including:
- The governments of Canada, India, S. Korea, Taiwan, Vietnam, USA
- The UN secretariat in Geneva
- The Association of South-East Asian Nations
- The International Olympic Committee and the World Anti-Doping Agency
- Defence contractors and hi-tech companies.

Worldwide, Capital One, 2019: Credit card company revealed a hacker accessed data on 100 million credit card applications, including applicants' bank account numbers.

Worldwide, Play Station, 2011: Cyber penetration of PlayStation network accessed personal data of more than 80 million users.

Worldwide, WannaCry, 2017: 150 countries hit by WannaCry ransomware that locked files and demanded ransom payment in Bitcoin. Russia, Ukraine, India, and Taiwan were most affected. UK health service, German railways and telecom companies in Argentina, Portugal, and Spain also hit hard.

Worldwide, Yahoo, 2013: The biggest ever (known) impact of a cyber breach: 3 billion personal records compromised in hack attack on Yahoo.

US Navy, June 2018: Chinese government hackers compromised the networks of a US Navy contractor, stealing 614 GB of data related to weapons, sensor, and communication systems under development for US submarines.

USA, Congressional elections, 2018: US Cyber Command blocked internet access of Russian company The Internet Research Agency, reportedly involved in disinformation operations during 2016 US Presidential election.

USA, Sony Corp, 2014: Cyber intrusion presumed to originate from North Korea broke into Sony emails and employee files and dumped them online.

USA, Cyber Command, 2010: New US Military Command was established under a Four Star General. 30,000 troops initially assigned; number as high as 60,000 by 2020.

USA, 2009: For the first time, Chinese government is identified as source of hacking attack on Google and 45 other US companies.

UK, Easyjet airline, May 2020: Chinese hackers accessed the travel records of 9 million customers of UK airline EasyJet.

Estonia, 2007: A series of a "distributed denial of service" (DDoS) attacks originating from Russia disrupted government departments and interrupted access to emergency services.

Copenhagen, NotPetya, 2017: Maersk shipping was the main target of NotPetya malware that temporarily shut down 76 ports and 800 ships, representing 18% of global cargo. The following year, UK and USA officially blamed NotPetya on Russia.

Brussels, European Union, 2018: The EU acknowledged China has had access to sensitive EU communications for several years.

London, UK, 2012: UK's counter-intelligence director illustrated cyber threat by reference to an unnamed major UK company that lost around $1.35bn in a hostile cyber attack.

Georgia, 2008: As the Russian–Georgian war started, Russian nationalists mounted a "distributed denial of service" (DDoS) attack on Georgia – flooding government websites with bogus enquiries so as to overwhelm and crash them.

Airbus, Europe, 2012: EADS (Airbus) and German steelmaker Thyssenkrupp recorded major attacks by Chinese hackers.

US military, Middle East, 2008: At a US military base in the Middle East, memory sticks containing a self-propagating worm were deliberately left in a washroom. One or more soldiers broke regulations by putting one in a military laptop. US Central Command was infected; the clean up took 14 months.

Egypt, 2019: Journalists, academics, lawyers, human rights activists, and opposition politicians suffered cyberattacks – widely assumed to be carried out by the government.

Syria, 2007: Syria defenceless against Israeli air strike because US Air Force software disabled Syrian air defence.

Saudi Arabia, 2012: Iranian Shamoon virus attacked Saudi Aramco oil company, shutting thousands of computers and hard drives, leaving image of burning American flag on many screens. Repeat attack in 2016.

Hong Kong, June 2019: A denial-of-service attack on encrypted messaging service Telegram disrupted communications among HK protesters.

Ukraine, 2016: Cyberattack on national power company shut down electricity in northern Kiev for 30 minutes.

Western Intelligence, 2018: Russian internet search company Yandex penetrated by hackers using software known to be used by the Five Eyes intelligence alliance of Australia, Canada, New Zealand, UK, and USA.

Iran, 2019: Allegations surfaced that Iranian hackers targeted over 170 universities worldwide, 2013–2017, stealing $3.4 billion worth of intellectual property.

Iran, 2010: US–Israeli-designed Stuxnet virus deactivated 30,000 Iranian government computers and a quarter of Iran's enrichment centrifuges.

Iran, 2012: Israel's Flamer cyber worm wiped out Iranian hard drives and forced cut in oil production.

Virtual manoeuvres, 2011, 2012: US and Chinese officials jointly played cyber war games.

South Korean military, 2016: US and South Korean contingency plans in the event of war accessed by hackers, allegedly from North Korea.

South Korea, Seoul, 2013: Computer networks of major banks and broadcasters were attacked by a virus designed to wipe out their stored data. North Korea widely blamed for attack, which occurred during joint US and South Korean military manoeuvres.

Huawei, 2019: Chinese telecoms mega-corporation accused US government of hacking into its internal information systems to disrupt business operations.

China, 2019: China's National Computer Network Emergency Response Technical Team claimed so many cyberattacks came from USA it was like all-out cyber war against China.

China, 2010: The government claimed it was hit by almost 500,000 cyberattacks – 15% from USA, 8% from India, approx. 25% from elsewhere outside China.

3D printing

Additive manufacturing (AM), generally known as 3D printing, creates three-dimensional objects. It is especially useful for producing prototypes, for making quick design changes, and potentially for making components that are no longer commercially available. 3D printing has been used to manufacture parts for weapons (see below), but during the Covid-19 crisis of 2020, the 3D printing community was quick to offer their technology for the rapid production of parts for ventilators and PPE.

Developments reported during 2010s

YEAR

2010s   50lb-warhead for hypersonic missile like the X51A Waverider is 3D-printed.

2010s   Los Alamos National Laboratory (site of original atomic bomb research in 1940s) pioneers 3D printing for high explosives to be used in US nuclear weapons.

2010s   Dutch researchers 3D-print TNT.

2013   A US student makes the first 3D-printed gun out of plastic and calls it "Liberator".

2013   NASA successfully tests a 3D-printed engine injector for a rocket – extra thrust with fewer components.

2014   The Sellafield (UK) nuclear plant 3D-prints a custom-designed lid for a nuclear waste container.

2015   Raytheon Corp (US) announces it has produced a missile in which 80% of components are 3D-printed.

The future:

- Bioprinting of human tissues offers medical opportunities but could also be used to transmit toxins for use as weapons.

- If digital files of small arms can be transmitted instead of the physical object having to be transported from one place to another, how will they be controlled?

Artificial intelligence and the arms race

Artificial intelligence (AI) and machine learning mean huge amounts of information can be handled much, much faster. Whether that is good or bad depends on how it is used.

For pre-emptive response to threats? For armed robots? For greater accuracy in missile strikes? For ensuring agreements and treaties are properly implemented? All are possible.

AI in attack and defence
Examples of areas in which it can be used

Early warning and intelligence, surveillance, reconnaissance (ISR)

- detection of enemy attack
- data processing and analysis
- predicting enemy's nuclear-related activity

Cyber security and attack

- better defence mechanisms against cyberattacks
- enhanced capability for cyberattacks

Nuclear and conventional weapons Autonomous:

- drones
- hypersonics
- surface and underwater vehicles

Defensive mechanisms

- better targeting of defensive systems
- better detection of enemy signals
- better jamming capabilities
- autonomous anti-submarine and counter-mine systems
- autonomous robots for protection of nuclear assets

Health of
the people

The health of the people reflects the health of a society. Good health is a basic need and access to good healthcare a basic right, a central part of the contract between state and citizen in many parts of the world. And the health of the people is a significant success story in the last century and a half of human development and progress. Despite the many flaws of modern society, more people live longer today than ever before, mainly because of better public health systems, clean water and safe sewage treatment, improved nutrition, and more medical knowledge and care. And yet...

It is not just the Covid-19 pandemic of 2020 that presses pause on relative optimism about the global health horizon. It is, however, an enormous wake-up call. Preparations were generally deficient, though warnings

had been sounded. Some governments' response to the pandemic has been tragically poor. Even where the response has been relatively effective, most countries have revealed their lack of resilience, often due to spending cuts in the previous decade. Care for the elderly, as a prime example, has been done as cheaply as possible.

The Covid-19 pandemic is the latest episode in a series of novel infectious diseases this century: SARS, MERS, H1N1, Ebola. The increasing tempo is worrying. And now the World Health Organization, riven by disputes, has been weakened by the USA deciding to withdraw its membership and funding.

The big killing diseases of our time, however, are lifestyle-related. While malnutrition and hunger are increasing

again, the food-related epidemic is obesity. Carrying too much body weight is a major health risk. Likewise smoking, also increasing, and a major cause of heart disease, respiratory disease and some kinds of cancer.

Yet cancer is in some ways a story that reflects progress; if caught early, most kinds of cancer are treatable. With HIV/AIDS, there has been progress; it cannot be cured but can be managed. But mental health remains a taboo issue in many countries – impossible to discuss and therefore impossible to manage, even if resources were available.

Overall, however, huge advances have been registered in public health and the treatment of diseases. The way we live continues to generate problems that medical science has to solve. The next step, surely, is to figure out how to live better.

Pandemics

The first identified cases of illness caused by a novel corona virus surfaced in Wuhan province in China in December 2019. In January 2020 it spread beyond China. At the end of the month, the World Health Organization called it a Public Health Emergency of International Concern. In February it named the new virus Covid-19 and during March labelled the outbreak a global pandemic.

Every day people read the Covid-19 statistics – the numbers of cases and deaths – watching them mount. All were misleading and incomplete. Much official data was an understatement and even when that was not

deliberate, counting methodologies differed markedly from one country to another.

Indirect consequences were also striking. Many countries introduced lockdowns, which slowed the rate of infection but had other consequences including a globally recorded upsurge in domestic violence. And with Covid-19 taking priority, many patients with other debilitating diseases went untreated.

Like the 21st century's other pandemics – and like 60% of known diseases and 75% of new ones – Covid-19 is probably zoonotic, meaning it was transmitted from animals to people.

The age of epidemics and pandemics

Countries worst affected

- SARS: Severe Acute Respiratory Syndrome (2002–2003)
- H1N1 (Swine flu) (2009–2010)
- MERS: Middle East Respiratory Syndrome (2012–2020)
- Ebola (2014–2016)
- Ebola (2018–2020)
- no data

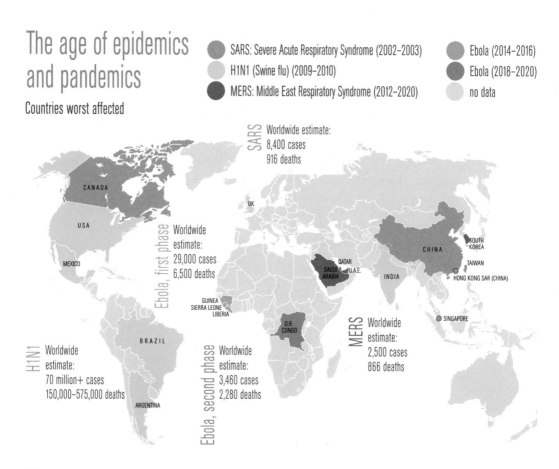

SARS Worldwide estimate:
8,400 cases
916 deaths

Ebola, first phase Worldwide estimate:
29,000 cases
6,500 deaths

H1N1 Worldwide estimate:
70 million+ cases
150,000–575,000 deaths

Ebola, second phase Worldwide estimate:
3,460 cases
2,280 deaths

MERS Worldwide estimate:
2,500 cases
866 deaths

CANADA
USA
MEXICO
BRAZIL
ARGENTINA
UK
GUINEA
SIERRA LEONE
LIBERIA
D.R. CONGO
QATAR
SAUDI ARABIA
U.A.E.
INDIA
CHINA
SOUTH KOREA
TAIWAN
HONG KONG SAR (CHINA)
SINGAPORE

Covid-19

Epicentres of the Covid-19 pandemic

January – June 2020

epicentres

other countries with confirmed cases of Covid-19

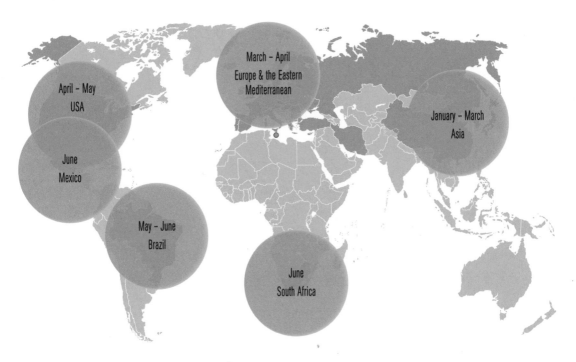

March – April
Europe & the Eastern Mediterranean

April – May
USA

June
Mexico

January – March
Asia

May – June
Brazil

June
South Africa

Covid-19 confirmed cases

By region

January – June 2020

- Americas
- Europe
- Eastern Mediterranean
- South-East Asia
- Africa
- Western Pacific

180,000
160,000
140,000
120,000
100,000
80,000
60,000
40,000
20,000
0

11 January   1 February   1 March   1 April   1 May   1 June   22 June

Malnutrition

USA More than 40 million people turn to the Feeding America network each year.

UK The Trussell Trust handed out 1.6 million three-day food packages in 2018/19.

Germany 1.65 million people relied on food donations in 2019, according to Tafel, the umbrella organization for food banks.

Undernourished people

Percentage of population whose food intake
is insufficient to meet dietary energy requirements
2017

- 40% or more
- 20% – 39%
- 5% – 19%
- fewer than 5%
- no data

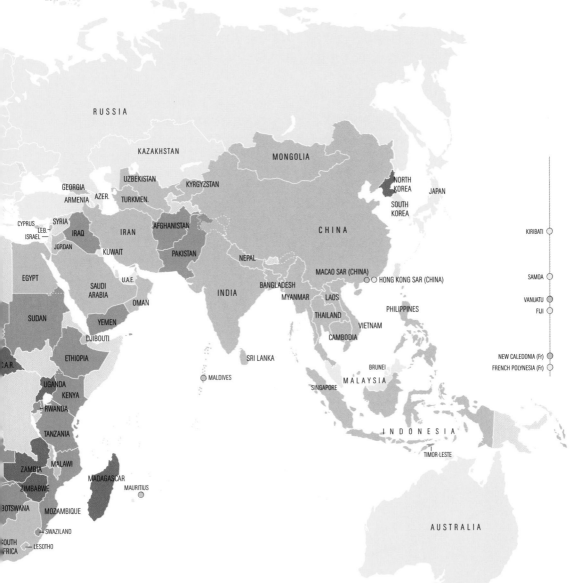

137

Undernourishment

From 2005 to 2015, the number of undernourished people worldwide decreased steadily. In 2015 that trend stopped and the number started to increase again, in line with the growing world population.

The main factors behind this reversal are climate change and violent conflict. However, shortages of food are caused by a range of different factors. People's ability to grow enough food can be hit by changes such as the length and timing of the rainy season due to climate change. People's ability to buy enough food can be hit by volatility in world food prices as a result of developments in far distant countries. Crop failure, natural disasters, and war have a heavy impact, as do structural economic deficiencies such as supply problems and poor local transport infrastructure.

Deficiencies in diet are as serious a problem as insufficiencies of food. The absence of vitamins in daily intake can lead to crushing ailments. Vitamin A deficiency, for instance, affects an estimated 250 million pre-school children and is the leading cause of preventable blindness in children as well as increasing the risk of disease and death from severe infections.

Hunger

Number of undernourished people 2005–2018

Latin America & Caribbean   Asia   Africa   — prevalence of global undernourishment

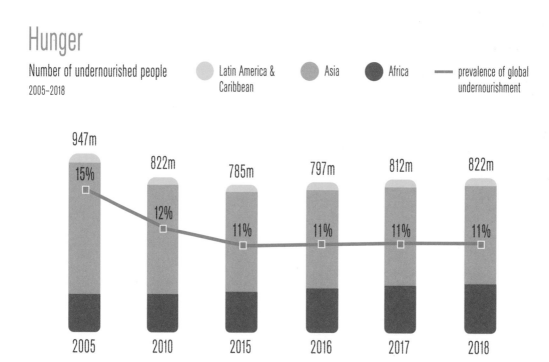

Food shortages

Requiring external assistance

as of September 2019

● exceptional shortage in food production/supplies

● severe but localized food insecurity

● widespread lack of access to basic food

● no food shortage requiring external assistance

NORTH KOREA

SYRIA
IRAQ
AFGHANISTAN
PAKISTAN
LIBYA
BANGLADESH
HAITI
CAPE VERDE
MAURITANIA
MALI
NIGER CHAD
SUDAN
ERITREA
YEMEN
DJIBOUTI
MYANMAR
VENEZUELA
SENEGAL
GUINEA
SIERRA LEONE
LIBERIA
NIGERIA
CAMEROON
C.A.R
SOUTH SUDAN
ETHIOPIA
SOMALIA
BURKINA FASO
CONGO
D.R. OF CONGO
UGANDA
KENYA
BURUNDI
MALAWI
MADAGASCAR
ZIMBABWE
MOZAMBIQUE
SWAZILAND
LESOTHO

Vitamin A deficiency affects around
250 million
pre-school children worldwide

Obesity

CANADA

USA

MEXICO

BELIZE
GUATEMALA
EL SALVADOR
HONDURAS
NICARAGUA
COSTA RICA
PANAMA

BAHAMAS
CUBA
JAMAICA
HAITI
DOMINICAN REP.

ST KITTS & NEVIS
ANTIGUA & BARBUDA
DOMINICA
ST LUCIA
GRENADA
BARBADOS
ST VINCENT & GRENADINES
TRINIDAD & TOBAGO

VENEZUELA
GUYANA
COLOMBIA
SURINAME

ECUADOR

PERU

BRAZIL

BOLIVIA

PARAGUAY

CHILE
ARGENTINA
URUGUAY

ICELAND
NORWAY
SWEDEN
FINL
UK
DENMARK
IRELAND
NETH.
BEL.
GERMANY
POLA
LUX.
CZ REP.
SLOVA
AUS.
HU
SW.
SL
FRANCE
CR. B P
MONT.
PORTUGAL
ANDORRA
SPAIN
ITALY
GI
TUNISIA
MALT.
MOROCCO
ALGERIA
LIBYA

CAPE VERDE
MAURITANIA
MALI
NIGER
CHI
SENEGAL
GAMBIA
BURKINA FASO
GUINEA-BISSAU
GUINEA
BENIN
NIGERIA
SIERRA LEONE
CÔTE D'IVOIRE
GHANA
TOGO
LIBERIA
C.A.R
CAMEROON
EQUATORIAL GUINEA
SÃO TOME & PRINCIPE
GABON
CONGO
CO

ANGO

NAMIBIA

Overweight adults

Percentage of adults with Body Mass
Index (BMI) of 25 or more

2016

66% or more

51% – 65%

31% – 50%

30% or fewer

no data

RUSSIA

BELARUS

UKRAINE

MOLDOVA

M.

UL

GEORGIA

REP. OF
TURKEY

ARMENIA

AZER.

CYPRUS
ISRAEL

LEB.

SYRIA

JORDAN

IRAQ

KUWAIT

BAHRAIN

QATAR

U.A.E.

EGYPT

SAUDI
ARABIA

OMAN

SUDAN

ERITREA

YEMEN

DJIBOUTI

SOUTH
SUDAN

ETHIOPIA

SOMALIA

UGANDA

KENYA

RWANDA

BURUNDI

TANZANIA

SEYCHELLES

COMOROS

ZAMBIA

MALAWI

ZIMBABWE

MADAGASCAR

MAURITIUS

JTSWANA

MOZAMBIQUE

OUTH
FRICA

SWAZILAND

LESOTHO

KAZAKHSTAN

UZBEKISTAN

KYRGYZSTAN

TURKMEN.

TAJIKISTAN

AFGHANISTAN

IRAN

PAKISTAN

MONGOLIA

NEPAL

BHUTAN

INDIA

BANGLADESH

MYANMAR

SRI LANKA

MALDIVES

CHINA

NORTH
KOREA

SOUTH
KOREA

JAPAN

LAOS

THAILAND

CAMBODIA

VIETNAM

PHILIPPINES

BRUNEI

MALAYSIA

SINGAPORE

INDONESIA

TIMOR-LESTE

PAPUA
NEW
GUINEA

SOLOMON
ISLANDS

AUSTRALIA

NEW
ZEALAND

MICRONESIA, FED. ST. OF

MARSHALL ISLANDS

PALAU

NAURU

KIRIBATI

TUVALU

SAMOA

VANUATU

FIJI

COOK IS. (NZ)

NIUE (NZ)

TONGA

Impact of obesity

The incidence of obesity has more than trebled since 1975. An estimated 1.9 billion adults in the world are overweight or obese. Most people live in countries where there are more deaths from excess weight than from undernourishment. A person carrying excessive body weight risks contracting a range of debilitating and life-threatening health conditions.

The problem is not just the amount of food that people eat but, to a much greater extent, what we eat. Cheap processed foods are particularly high in animal fats and sugars. They make an affordable diet for people on low incomes but directly fuel the obesity epidemic. Worldwide, health services are struggling to cope with the strain.

Overweight as cause of death

Percentage of deaths from common causes
attributable to a Body Mass Index (BMI) of 25 or more
2017

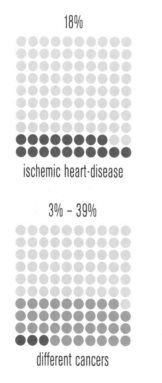

18%

ischemic heart-disease

3% – 39%

different cancers

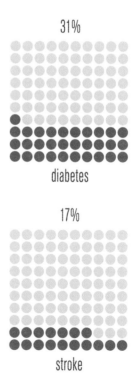

31%

diabetes

17%

stroke

America's growing obesity problem

Percentage of population in each state
reported as having a BMI of 30 or more

2012, 2015, 2018

● 35.0% or more   ● 30.0% – 34.9%   ● 25.0% – 29.9%   ○ less than 25.0%

Smoking

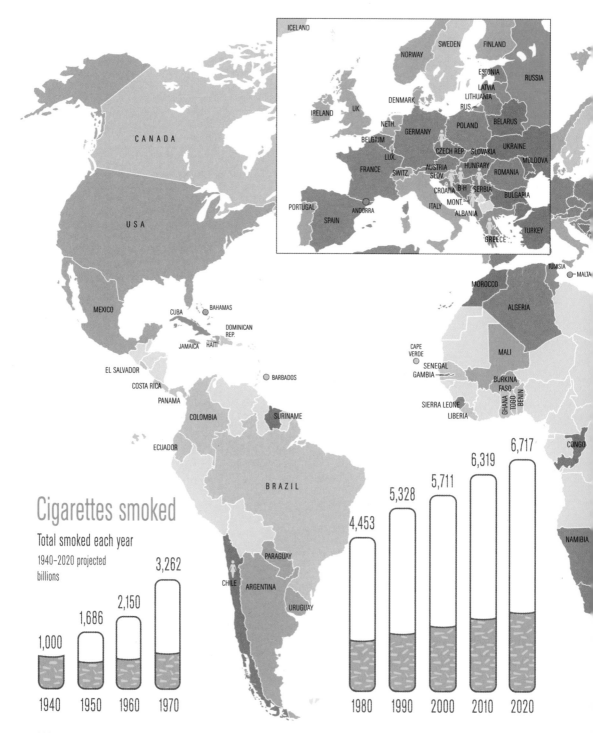

ICELAND

NORWAY   SWEDEN   FINLAND

ESTONIA   RUSSIA
LATVIA
LITHUANIA
DENMARK   RUS.
IRELAND   UK   NETH.   POLAND   BELARUS
BELGIUM   GERMANY   UKRAINE
LUX.   CZECH REP   SLOVAKIA   MOLDOVA
FRANCE   SWITZ.   AUSTRIA   HUNGARY   ROMANIA
SLOV   B-H   SERBIA   BULGARIA
PORTUGAL   CROATIA   MONT.   ALBANIA
SPAIN   ANDORRA   ITALY   TURKEY
GREECE

CANADA

USA

MEXICO   CUBA   BAHAMAS
DOMINICAN REP.
JAMAICA   HAITI
EL SALVADOR   BARBADOS
COSTA RICA
PANAMA
COLOMBIA
SURINAME
ECUADOR

BRAZIL

PARAGUAY
CHILE   ARGENTINA
URUGUAY

TUNISIA   MALTA
MOROCCO
ALGERIA
CAPE VERDE   MALI
SENEGAL
GAMBIA   BURKINA FASO
SIERRA LEONE   GHANA TOGO BENIN
LIBERIA   CONGO

NAMIBIA

Cigarettes smoked

Total smoked each year

1940–2020 projected
billions

1,000   1940
1,686   1950
2,150   1960
3,262   1970
4,453   1980
5,328   1990
5,711   2000
6,319   2010
6,717   2020

144

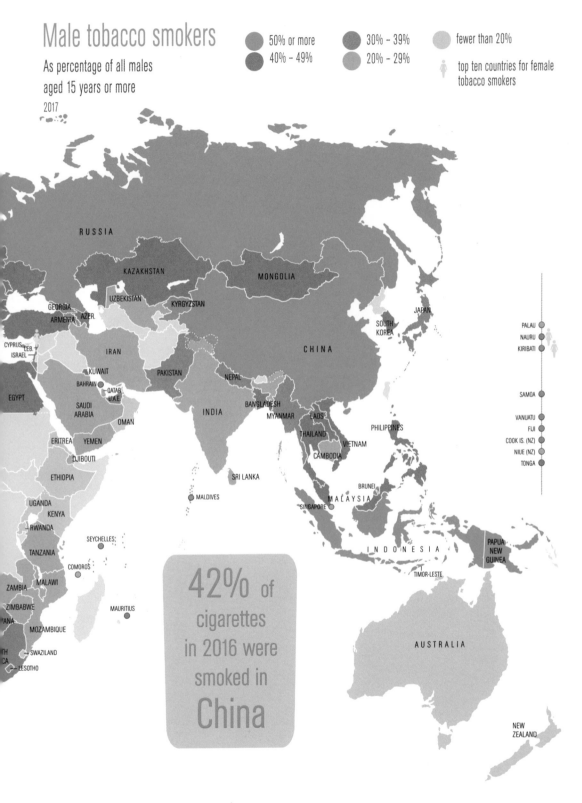

Male tobacco smokers

As percentage of all males
aged 15 years or more

2017

50% or more
40% – 49%
30% – 39%
20% – 29%
fewer than 20%
top ten countries for female tobacco smokers

42% of cigarettes in 2016 were smoked in **China**

RUSSIA
KAZAKHSTAN
MONGOLIA
UZBEKISTAN
KYRGYZSTAN
GEORGIA
ARMENIA   AZER.
CYPRUS LEB.
ISRAEL
IRAN
EGYPT
KUWAIT
BAHRAIN   QATAR
SAUDI   U.A.E.
ARABIA
OMAN
ERITREA YEMEN
DJIBOUTI
ETHIOPIA
UGANDA
KENYA
RWANDA
TANZANIA
ZAMBIA   MALAWI
ZIMBABWE
...ANA
MOZAMBIQUE
..TH
CA
SWAZILAND
LESOTHO
SEYCHELLES
COMOROS
MAURITIUS
PAKISTAN
NEPAL
INDIA
BANGLADESH
MYANMAR
SRI LANKA
MALDIVES
CHINA
JAPAN
SOUTH
KOREA
LAOS
THAILAND
VIETNAM
CAMBODIA
PHILIPPINES
BRUNEI
MALAYSIA
SINGAPORE
INDONESIA
TIMOR-LESTE
PAPUA
NEW
GUINEA
AUSTRALIA
NEW
ZEALAND

PALAU
NAURU
KIRIBATI
SAMOA
VANUATU
FIJI
COOK IS. (NZ)
NIUE (NZ)
TONGA

145

Smoke-free legislation

March 2019

- all public places smoke-free, or at least 90% of population covered by complete subnational smoke-free legislation
- comprehensive smoke-free law, including bars and restaurants
- no effective legislation

Tobacco-related deaths

Per year

2005–08, 2009–2030 projected

— total   — developing countries   — developed countries

5.4   5.9   6.5

3.8   4.3   4.9

1.6   1.6   1.6

9 million
8 million
7 million
6 million
5 million
4 million
3 million
2 million
1 million

2005   2010   2015

RUSSIA

MARSHALL ISLANDS ◉

NAURU ◉

NIUE (NZ) ◉

MALTA
TURKEY   TURKMEN.
LEBANON   TAJIKISTAN
PALESTINE   IRAN   AFGHANISTAN

LIBYA   EGYPT   PAKISTAN   NEPAL

CHAD   LAOS
                                  THAILAND
                                  CAMBODIA

UGANDA   BRUNEI

CONGO

BURUNDI   SEYCHELLES ◉   PAPUA
                                                     NEW
                                                     GUINEA   8.2

MADAGASCAR   7.6
AMIBIA   BOTSWANA   7   6.8
                          5.4   6.1
                                                     AUSTRALIA

                                              NEW
                                              ZEALAND
            1.5   1.5   1.4

2020   2025   2030

Cancer

Cancer is a generic name for diseases characterized by the growth and spread of abnormal cells. It is the second leading cause of death, responsible for 16 per cent of all deaths. Though treatments and preventive strategies are improving, the incidence of cancer more than doubled from 1975 to 2008 and grew by 42 per cent in the subsequent 10 years.

As the world's population grows, and improvements in general health mean that people live longer on average, cancer looms ever larger. In countries where prosperity is advancing, bringing with it changes in lifestyle, diet, and tobacco use, the incidence of cancer is rising. Although the rate of cancer is currently 2.5 times greater in high-income countries than elsewhere, rates in poorer countries are increasing rapidly.

Cancer is most treatable when caught early. On a large scale, early diagnosis requires education and active screening programmes as part of comprehensive health care – more likely prospects in richer than in poorer countries.

Cancer on the increase

Number of new cases globally per year
1975, 2008, 2012, 2018, 2040 projected

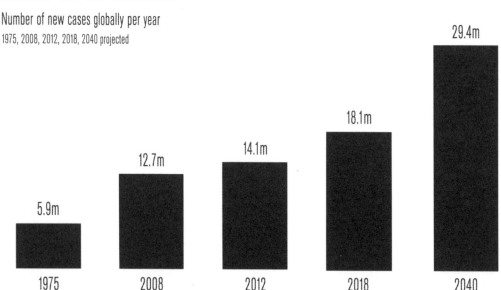

5.9m	12.7m	14.1m	18.1m	29.4m
1975	2008	2012	2018	2040

Childhood-cancer survival rates

Observed in cases diagnosed with lymphoid leukemia

2018

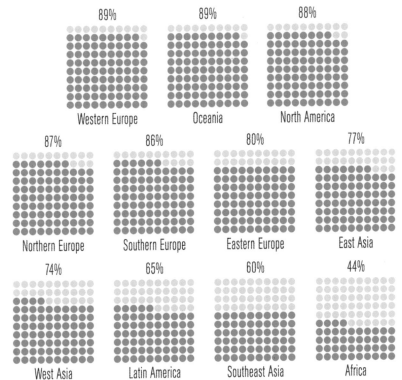

89% Western Europe

89% Oceania

88% North America

87% Northern Europe

86% Southern Europe

80% Eastern Europe

77% East Asia

74% West Asia

65% Latin America

60% Southeast Asia

44% Africa

Environmental factors

Contributing to development of cancer

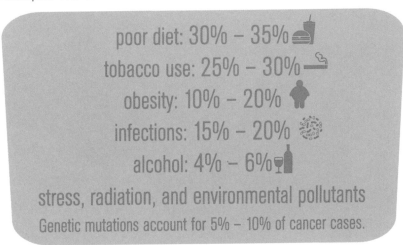

poor diet: 30% – 35%

tobacco use: 25% – 30%

obesity: 10% – 20%

infections: 15% – 20%

alcohol: 4% – 6%

stress, radiation, and environmental pollutants

Genetic mutations account for 5% – 10% of cancer cases.

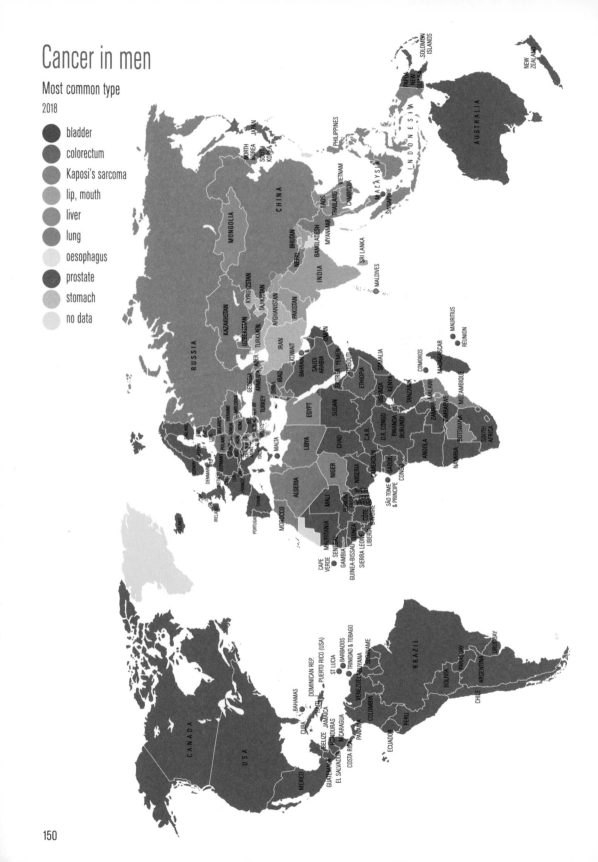

Cancer in men

Most common type

2018

- bladder
- colorectum
- Kaposi's sarcoma
- lip, mouth
- liver
- lung
- oesophagus
- prostate
- stomach
- no data

Cancer in women

Most common type

2018

- breast
- cervix
- liver
- thyroid
- no data

HIV/AIDS

ICELAND

NORWAY

FINLAND

ESTONIA

LATVIA

DENMARK

IRELAND

BELARUS

GERMANY

UKRAINE

CZECH REP. SLOVAKIA

MOLDOVA

LUX.

HUNGARY

ROMANIA

FRANCE

SLOV.

CROATIA B-H SERBIA

BULGARIA

ITALY MONT.

PORTUGAL

N. MAC., REP. OF

SPAIN

TUNISIA

MOROCCO

MEXICO

ALGERIA

LIBYA

BAHAMAS

CUBA

DOMINICAN
REP.

HAITI

CAPE
VERDE

MAURITANIA

MALI

NIGER

CHAD

BELIZE

JAMAICA

SENEGAL

GUATEMALA

HONDURAS

GAMBIA

BURKINA
FASO

NIGERIA

EL SALVADOR

ST KITTS & NEVIS

GUINEA-BISSAU

GUINEA

NICARAGUA

CÔTE
D'IVOIRE

GHANA
TOGO
BENIN

COSTA RICA

BARBADOS

SIERRA LEONE

CAMEROON

C.A.R.

ST VINCENT & GRENADINES

LIBERIA

PANAMA

EQUATORIAL
GUINEA

GUYANA

COLOMBIA

SURINAME

GABON

D.R.
CONG

ECUADOR

CONGO

PERU

BRAZIL

AIDS orphans

ANGOLA

𝍫 100,000

BOLIVIA

NAMIBIA

PARAGUAY

BOTSWAN

CHILE

ARGENTINA

SOU
AFRI

URUGUAY

Impact of HIV/AIDS

Percentage of people
age 15–49 living with HIV
2018

20.0% – 28.0%

10.0% – 19.9%

1.0% – 9.9%

less than 1.0%

no data

Barring the door

OMAN country imposing restrictions on entry, stay,
or residence of people living with HIV
2018

HIV/AIDS treatment

HIV/AIDS has claimed around 32 million lives over nearly four decades. In 2018, there were nearly 40 million people living with HIV.

A cure for HIV infection has not been found, but anti-retroviral therapy (ART) drugs enable people to live a healthy and productive life. ART can also stop transmission of HIV from mother to unborn child and has prevented more than 1.6 million children from becoming infected. The drugs are, however, by no means universally available.

Neither denying the problem nor trying to bar the door to people living with HIV/AIDS (as 44 countries still do) has worked as a preventive strategy. But, thanks to treatment and education, the numbers of new infections and deaths are declining. So, the epidemic can be stopped – but only if more resources are provided to fight it.

HIV/AIDS over time

Among adults and children
1990–2018

—— number newly infected with HIV
—— number of deaths

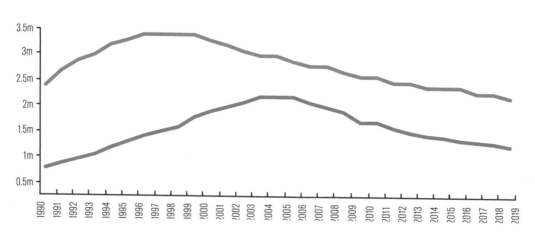

Anti-retroviral therapy (ART)

People receiving ART as
percentage of adults and children
living with HIV

2018

○ number of adults and children living with HIV/AIDS

● percentage receiving ART

1.7m

38%

Eastern Europe and Central Asia

5.9m

54%

Asia and the Pacific

0.2m

 32%

Middle East and North Africa

2.2m

62%

Latin American and Caribbean

5m

51%

Western and Central Africa

20.6m

67%

Eastern and Southern Africa

2.2m

79%

Western and Central Europe and North America

Mental health

Worldwide, around one person in 10 is estimated to be living with a mental health disorder at any time. In all, around one in four people will be affected by mental or neurological disorders at some point in their lives.

The majority who suffer from poor mental health experience anxiety and depression; women are more likely to be affected than men. Growing numbers of children and adolescents have mental health problems of some degree; about half of mental disorders begin before the age of 14.

People with mental disorders are at greater risk of catching and passing on communicable diseases, and of suicide. About 800,000 people take their own lives each year. Suicide is the third leading cause of death among young people.

In many countries, mental disorder is a taboo subject, more shaming to a family than other diseases or abnormal behaviours. Stigma leads to this large and highly visible health issue being under-resourced and to the human rights of psychiatric patients being routinely abused in most countries. Average global spending on mental health is less than $2 per person per year; in high-income countries, where there remain criticisms and complaints that provision for this aspect of health is not adequate, the level of spending per person is 4,000 times the level in low-income countries.

Mental health disorders

Number of people worldwide estimated to have disorder
2017

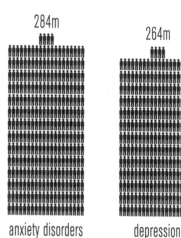

284m

anxiety disorders

264m

depression

46m

bipolar disorder

20m

schizophrenia

16m

eating disorders

Spending on mental health

Median government expenditure in US$ on
mental health per capita
2016

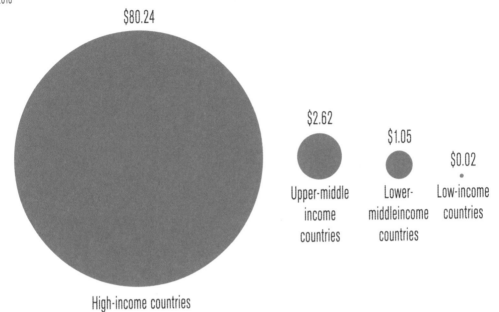

$80.24

High-income countries

$2.62

Upper-middle
income
countries

$1.05

Lower-
middleincome
countries

$0.02

Low-income
countries

Psychiatrists per
million people:
High-income countries:
127
Low-income countries:
1

Suicide by men

Number of suicides per million men

2016

- 250 or more
- 100 – 249
- 50 – 99
- fewer than 50
- no data

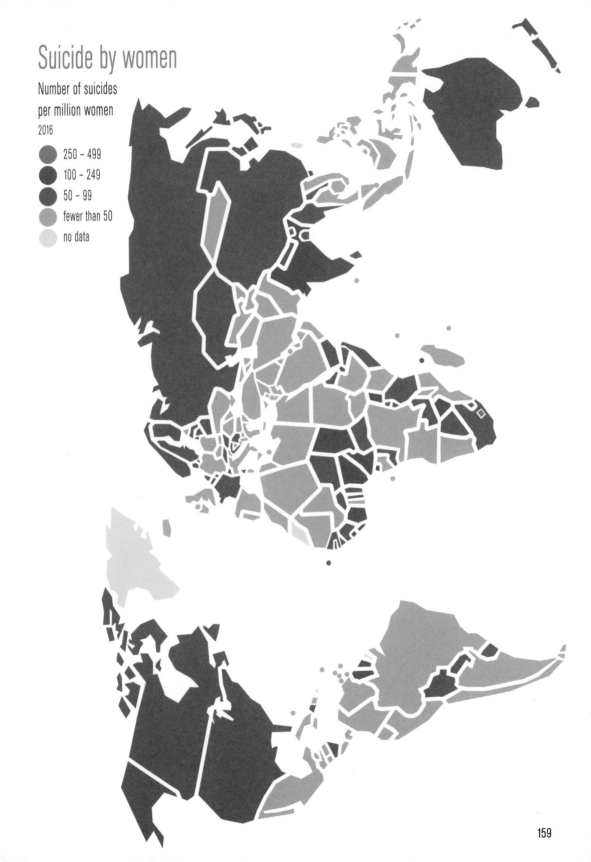

Suicide by women

Number of suicides
per million women
2016

- 250 – 499
- 100 – 249
- 50 – 99
- fewer than 50
- no data

Water and sanitation

ICELAND
GREENLAND (Den)
NORWAY
SWEDEN
FINLAND
ESTONIA
RUSSIA
LATVIA
LITHUANIA
DENMARK
RUS.
IRELAND
UK
NETH.
BELARUS
GERMANY
POLAND
BELGIUM
UKRAINE
LUX.
CZECH REP.
SLOVAKIA
MOLDOVA
FRANCE
SWITZ.
AUSTRIA
HUNGARY
ROMANIA
SLOV.
PORTUGAL
CROATIA
B.-H.
SERBIA
BULGARIA
ITALY
MONT.
SPAIN
ALBANIA
F.N. MAC. REP OF
TURKEY
GREECE

CANADA

USA

BERMUDA (UK)

TURKS & CAICOS IS. (UK)
DOMINICAN
REP.
MEXICO
BAHAMAS
CUBA
HAITI
PUERTO RICO (USA)
ANTIGUA & BARBUDA
GUADELOUPE (Fr)
MARTINIQUE (Fr)
GRENADA
BARBADOS
ST VINCENT & GRENADINES
TRINIDAD & TOBAGO
BELIZE
JAMAICA
GUATEMALA
HONDURAS
EL SALVADOR
NICARAGUA
COSTA RICA
PANAMA
VENEZUELA
GUYANA
SURINAME
FRENCH GUIANA (Fr)
ECUADOR
PERU
BRAZIL
BOLIVIA
PARAGUAY
CHILE
URUGUAY

TUNISIA
MOROCCO
ALGERIA
LIBYA
CAPE
VERDE
MAURITANIA
MALI
NIGER
SENEGAL
GAMBIA
BURKINA
CHAD
GUINEA-BISSAU
GUINEA
FASO
NIGERIA
SIERRA LEONE
CÔTE
GHANA
TOGO
BENIN
D'IVOIRE
LIBERIA
CAMEROON
EQUATORIAL
GUINEA
SÃO TOME
GABON
& PRINCIPE
D.R
CONGO
CON
ANGOLA
NAMIBIA
BOTSWA
SOUT
AFRI

Around 2 billion people gained access to an improved source of water between 1990 and 2010. Nonetheless, around 844 million people still lacked a basic drinking water supply in 2015.

They have to get their water from unprotected wells and springs, which often involves women and girls – who do most of this work – walking a long way, sometimes in dangerous conditions.

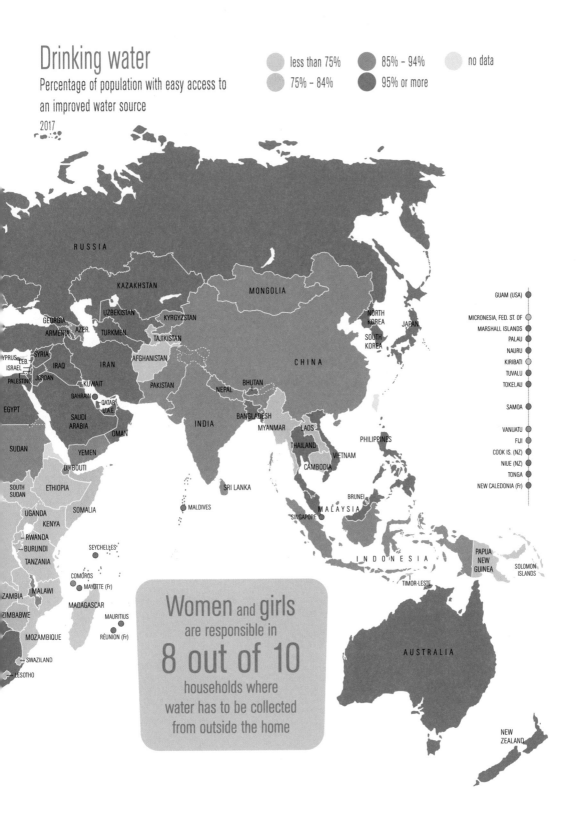

Drinking water

Percentage of population with easy access to
an improved water source

2017

less than 75%

75% – 84%

85% – 94%

95% or more

no data

RUSSIA

KAZAKHSTAN

MONGOLIA

GEORGIA

UZBEKISTAN

KYRGYZSTAN

NORTH
KOREA

JAPAN

ARMENIA

AZER.

TURKMEN.

SOUTH
KOREA

CYPRUS

LEB.

SYRIA

TAJIKISTAN

ISRAEL

IRAQ

IRAN

AFGHANISTAN

CHINA

PALESTINE

JORDAN

KUWAIT

BAHRAIN

QATAR

PAKISTAN

NEPAL

BHUTAN

U.A.E.

EGYPT

SAUDI
ARABIA

OMAN

INDIA

BANGLADESH

MYANMAR

LAOS

THAILAND

VIETNAM

PHILIPPINES

SUDAN

YEMEN

CAMBODIA

DJIBOUTI

SOUTH
SUDAN

ETHIOPIA

SRI LANKA

BRUNEI

UGANDA

SOMALIA

MALDIVES

MALAYSIA

KENYA

SINGAPORE

RWANDA

BURUNDI

SEYCHELLES

TANZANIA

INDONESIA

PAPUA
NEW
GUINEA

SOLOMON
ISLANDS

COMOROS

ZAMBIA

MALAWI

MAYOTTE (Fr)

MADAGASCAR

TIMOR-LESTE

ZIMBABWE

MAURITIUS

MOZAMBIQUE

RÉUNION (Fr)

AUSTRALIA

SWAZILAND

LESOTHO

GUAM (USA)

MICRONESIA, FED. ST. OF

MARSHALL ISLANDS

PALAU

NAURU

KIRIBATI

TUVALU

TOKELAU

SAMOA

VANUATU

FIJI

COOK IS. (NZ)

NIUE (NZ)

TONGA

NEW CALEDONIA (Fr)

NEW
ZEALAND

Women and girls are responsible in 8 out of 10 households where water has to be collected from outside the home

Sanitation

Percentage of population with access to basic sanitation facilities

2017

Legend:
- less than 25%
- 25% – 49%
- 50% – 74%
- 75% – 99%
- 99% or more
- no data

Safe management of human waste is crucial in the battle against many infectious diseases. At a basic level, people should not come into contact with human faeces, and facilities should ideally not be shared by more than one household.

Water is not essential to the disposal of human waste, but hand washing is an effective way of reducing the spread of disease. In 30 countries, more than half of all schools lack suitable lavatory facilities.

Unsafe schools

🙁 50% or more of schools have no drinking water, sanitation, or hand-washing facilities

2016

RUSSIA

KAZAKHSTAN

MONGOLIA

UZBEKISTAN

KYRGYZSTAN

GEORGIA

ARMENIA   AZER.   TURKMEN.   🙁 TAJIKISTAN

NORTH KOREA

JAPAN

MARSHALL ISLANDS ●

SOUTH KOREA

CYPRUS   LEB.
ISRAEL   SYRIA   IRAQ   IRAN   AFGHANISTAN

CHINA

KIRIBATI ●
TUVALU ●

PALESTINE   JORDAN

KUWAIT

PAKISTAN

NEPAL   BHUTAN

AMERICAN SAMOA (USA) ●

EGYPT

BAHRAIN ●
QATAR
U.A.E

SAUDI ARABIA

OMAN

INDIA

BANGLADESH

MYANMAR

🙁 LAOS

HONG KONG SAR (CHINA)

VANUATU ●

🙁 SUDAN

🙁 YEMEN

THAILAND

PHILIPPINES

TONGA ●

DJIBOUTI

🙁 VIETNAM

SOUTH SUDAN   🙁 ETHIOPIA

🙁 CAMBODIA

🙁 UGANDA   🙁 SOMALIA

SRI LANKA

KENYA

MALDIVES ●

MALAYSIA

🙁 RWANDA
🙁 BURUNDI

SINGAPORE

TANZANIA

I N D O N E S I A

PAPUA NEW GUINEA

🙁 SOLOMON ISLANDS

🙁 COMOROS

TIMOR-LESTE

ZAMBIA   🙁 MALAWI

🙁 MADAGASCAR

AUSTRALIA

ZIMBABWE

🙁 MOZAMBIQUE

SWAZILAND

LESOTHO

In 24 countries,
more than 20% of people
have to defecate
in the open,
which poses great health risks
to the community

NEW ZEALAND

Living with disease

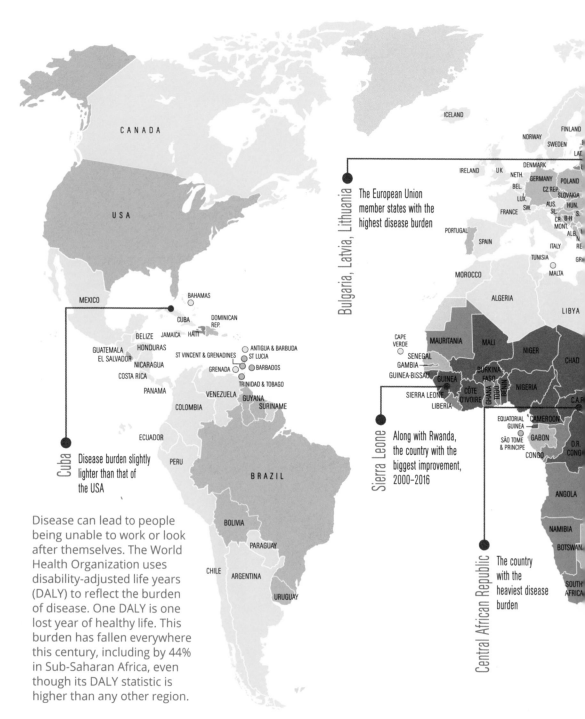

CANADA

ICELAND

NORWAY
FINLAND
SWEDEN
LAT.

IRELAND   UK   NETH.   DENMARK
BEL.   GERMANY   POLAND
LUX.   CZ.REP.   SLOVAKIA
FRANCE   SW.   AUS.   HUN.
SL.   CR. B-H.
MONT.
ALB.
PORTUGAL   N.
SPAIN   ITALY   RE.
TUNISIA   GR.
MOROCCO   MALTA

ALGERIA   LIBYA

Bulgaria, Latvia, Lithuania
The European Union member states with the highest disease burden

USA

BAHAMAS

MEXICO

CUBA   DOMINICAN REP.
BELIZE   JAMAICA   HAITI
GUATEMALA   HONDURAS   ANTIGUA & BARBUDA
EL SALVADOR   ST VINCENT & GRENADINES   ST LUCIA
NICARAGUA   GRENADA   BARBADOS
COSTA RICA   TRINIDAD & TOBAGO
PANAMA   VENEZUELA   GUYANA
COLOMBIA   SURINAME

CAPE VERDE   MAURITANIA   MALI   NIGER   CHAD
SENEGAL
GAMBIA   BURKINA
GUINEA-BISSAU   GUINEA   FASO   NIGERIA
SIERRA LEONE   CÔTE   GHANA   BENIN
D'IVOIRE   TOGO   C.A.R
LIBERIA   EQUATORIAL   CAMEROON
GUINEA
SÃO TOME   GABON   D.R.
& PRINCIPE   CONGO   CONGO

ECUADOR

Cuba
Disease burden slightly lighter than that of the USA

PERU

BRAZIL

Sierra Leone
Along with Rwanda, the country with the biggest improvement, 2000–2016

ANGOLA

NAMIBIA

BOTSWANA

Disease can lead to people being unable to work or look after themselves. The World Health Organization uses disability-adjusted life years (DALY) to reflect the burden of disease. One DALY is one lost year of healthy life. This burden has fallen everywhere this century, including by 44% in Sub-Saharan Africa, even though its DALY statistic is higher than any other region.

BOLIVIA
PARAGUAY
CHILE   ARGENTINA
URUGUAY

SOUTH AFRICA

Central African Republic
The country with the heaviest disease burden

National disease burden

DALYs per 100 people

2016

60 – 91

45 – 59

30 – 44

15 – 29

A DALY (disability-adjusted life year) measures the number of years lost due to ill-health, disability, or early death.

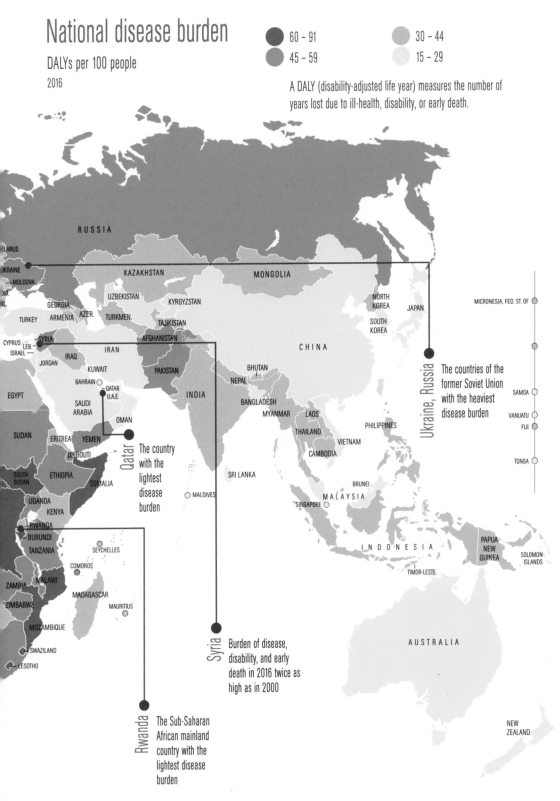

BELARUS

UKRAINE

MOLDOVA

OM.

IL.

RUSSIA

KAZAKHSTAN

MONGOLIA

GEORGIA

TURKEY

ARMENIA

AZER.

UZBEKISTAN

KYRGYZSTAN

NORTH KOREA

JAPAN

MICRONESIA, FED. ST. OF

CYPRUS

LEB.

ISRAEL

SYRIA

TURKMEN.

TAJIKISTAN

SOUTH KOREA

IRAN

AFGHANISTAN

CHINA

JORDAN

IRAQ

KUWAIT

BAHRAIN

QATAR

U.A.E.

PAKISTAN

BHUTAN

NEPAL

SAMOA

EGYPT

SAUDI ARABIA

OMAN

INDIA

BANGLADESH

MYANMAR

LAOS

VANUATU

FIJI

Qatar The country with the lightest disease burden

SUDAN

ERITREA

YEMEN

DJIBOUTI

THAILAND

VIETNAM

CAMBODIA

PHILIPPINES

Ukraine, Russia The countries of the former Soviet Union with the heaviest disease burden

TONGA

SOUTH SUDAN

ETHIOPIA

SOMALIA

SRI LANKA

MALDIVES

BRUNEI

MALAYSIA

SINGAPORE

UGANDA

KENYA

RWANDA

BURUNDI

TANZANIA

SEYCHELLES

COMOROS

I N D O N E S I A

PAPUA NEW GUINEA

SOLOMON ISLANDS

ZAMBIA

MALAWI

MADAGASCAR

MAURITIUS

TIMOR-LESTE

ZIMBABWE

MOZAMBIQUE

Syria Burden of disease, disability, and early death in 2016 twice as high as in 2000

AUSTRALIA

SWAZILAND

LESOTHO

Rwanda The Sub-Saharan African mainland country with the lightest disease burden

NEW ZEALAND

Health of the planet

Humanity has made a serious mess of our relationship with nature. The past 200 years have generated extraordinary progress, as more people live longer lives than ever before; and for many those longer lives are better than our forebears enjoyed. But that success is working against us.

The extent of human activity is extraordinary: 75 per cent of land surface has been significantly altered and we have had a major effect on 66 per cent of ocean area. Over 85 per cent of wetlands have been lost. With this, our species puts others at risk; the current decline in biodiversity is historically unprecedented.

Soaring economic output has pumped billions of tonnes of carbon dioxide and other greenhouse gases into the atmosphere; the laws of physics say that will increase average global temperatures with consequent changes in climate – and that is what is happening.

We have also pumped out noxious substances, creating a global crisis of air pollution that is exacerbated by the warming atmosphere. Our increasing output has generated enormous amounts of waste, often not disposed of responsibly, and we can see the consequences with our own eyes. And we are using (and wasting) more water than we can afford to: half the world's population will face water scarcity in the coming decade.

These things we know but we do not yet know how these environmental issues interact. Nature is essential for our existence and for a decent quality of life yet we have treated it with ignorant, clumsy disdain. We have tried to conquer nature while never ceasing to rely on it.

Awareness of our environmental predicament is rising. Action is being taken on different fronts: bans on plastic bags; state-funded incentives for low-carbon infrastructure; protecting sea and land areas from industrial intrusion; funding ecological restoration. These actions need to go further, faster. And they need to be knitted together by international cooperation.

The difficulty is that the most far-reaching and beneficial measures require deep changes in how our economy works and in our attitudes to consumption and waste. Many will oppose changes they see as weakening their privileges. Yet they too are part of nature; their well-being is also at stake. The tools are there. What is needed now is the intelligence and will to pick them up and use them.

Beyond the bounds

In this age of more, most, and never before, humanity is getting to the limit of the planet's hospitability to us. Our impact on the natural environment increases as the global population grows, and as industry and agriculture grow with it, along with consumption and extraction of natural resources.

Because it is unprecedented, the full consequences of humanity's impact on the environment are unknown. It is not clear how far we can go before the consequences get very serious. And compared to how much is already known about climate change, biodiversity loss, and other issues, not much at all is known about the interaction between the impacts.

A multinational group of scientists devised the concept of planetary boundaries to quantify how close we are to danger. The boundaries have not all been calculated and not every scientist agrees with the concept, the definitions, or the calculations. But the idea brings the key issues into sharp relief. Inside the boundaries, humanity is operating more or less safely. If we cross them, we don't know what will unfold. According to these scientists, we have crossed five boundaries, and in two cases have moved into the high-risk zone. There is time to ensure we do not cross more.

Boundary dimensions

	Measured by:	Boundary calculated as:
Biosphere integrity	Functional diversity	Not yet assessed
	Genetic diversity	Extinction rate of fewer than 10 extinctions per million species years
Climate change	Carbon dioxide in atmosphere	350 parts per million
Ocean acidification	Aragonite depletion in ocean	Reduction to not less than 80% of pre-industrial level
Stratospheric ozone depletion	Concentration of ozone in stratosphere	No more than 5% reduction from pre-industrial level
Biogeochemical flows	Phosphorus flow into oceans	11 million tonnes per year
	Nitrogen removed from atmosphere	62 million tonnes per year
Freshwater use	Maximum amount used	4,000 cubic kilometres per year
Land-system change	Area of forested land as % of original forest cover	75% of land surface
Atmospheric aerosol loading	Particles in the atmosphere	Not yet calculated
Novel entities		Not yet calculated

novel entities
not yet quantified

atmospheric aerosol loading
not yet quantified

Planetary boundaries

Assessment of the extent to which safe operating levels have
been reached or transgressed on selected impacts

2015

safe operating space

zone of uncertainty (increasing risk)

high-risk zone

boundary of safe operating space

boundary of uncertainty

biosphere integrity

genetic diversity

functional diversity
no global
quantification

climate change

ocean acidification
not yet quantified

stratospheric ozone depletion

phosphorus

nitrogen

biogeochemical flows

system change

freshwater use

Biodiversity loss

GREELAND

ICELAND
FAROE IS.

CANADA

NORWAY
FINLAND
SWEDEN ES
DENMARK LA
LITH
IRELAND
UK
NETH. GERMANY POLAND
BEL. CZ REP
LUX. SLOVAKIA
FRANCE SW. AUS. HUN.
SL.
ITALY CR. B H
PORTUGAL MONT. ALB
N. MAC., REP OF
SPAIN GREEC
TUNISIA MALTA
MOROCCO

USA

BERMUDA (UK)

TURKS & CAICOS IS. (UK)
BAHAMAS
CUBA
DOMINICAN
REP
HAITI
PUERTO RICO (USA)
ANTIGUA & BARBUDA
MEXICO
ST KITTS & NEVIS
GUADELOUPE (Fr)
DOMINICA
BELIZE JAMAICA
ST LUCIA
GUATEMALA HONDURAS
BARBADOS
EL SALVADOR
GRENADA ST VINCENT & GRENADINES
NICARAGUA
TRINIDAD & TOBAGO
COSTA RICA
PANAMA

VENEZUELA
GUYANA
COLOMBIA SURINAME
FRENCH GUIANA (Fr)

ECUADOR

PERU
BRAZIL

BOLIVIA

PARAGUAY

CHILE
ARGENTINA

URUGUAY

FALKLANDS IS. (UK)

WESTERN
SAHARA (Mor.)
ALGERIA
LIBYA

CAPE
VERDE MAURITANIA MALI NIGER CHAD
SENEGAL BURKINA
GAMBIA FASO NIGERIA
GUINEA-BISSAU GUINEA CÔTE
SIERRA LEONE D'IVOIRE
GHANA
TOGO
BENIN
CAMEROON C.A.R.
LIBERIA
EQUATORIAL
GUINEA GABON
SÃO TOME D.R.
& PRINCIPE CONGO
CONGO

ANGOLA

SAINT HELENA, ASCENSION AND
TRISTAN DA CUNHA

NAMIBIA
BOTSWAN

SOUTH
AFRICA

ANTARCTICA

Threatened mammals, birds, and amphibians

Number of species threatened
2019

- 100 or more
- 50 – 99
- 25 – 49
- 10 – 24
- fewer than 10
- no data

more than 50 species
of bird threatened

more than 50 species
of amphibian threatened

more than 50 species
of mammal threatened

RUSSIA

BELARUS
UKRAINE
MOLDOVA

KAZAKHSTAN

MONGOLIA

UZBEKISTAN
KYRGYZSTAN

GEORGIA
ARMENIA AZER. TURKMEN.
TURKEY
TAJIKISTAN

CYPRUS
SYRIA LEB.
ISRAEL IRAQ IRAN
PALESTINE JORDAN

AFGHANISTAN

NORTH
KOREA

JAPAN

SOUTH
KOREA

CHINA

KUWAIT
BAHRAIN QATAR
U.A.E.

PAKISTAN

NEPAL BHUTAN

TAIWAN

EGYPT

SAUDI
ARABIA

OMAN

INDIA

MACAO SAR (CHINA)

HONG KONG SAR (CHINA)

BANGLADESH
MYANMAR

SUDAN ERITREA YEMEN

DJIBOUTI

LAOS
THAILAND

VIETNAM

PHILIPPINES

SOUTH
SUDAN ETHIOPIA

SRI LANKA

CAMBODIA

BRUNEI

GUAM (USA)
NORTHERN MARIANA IS. (USA)
MICRONESIA, FED. ST. OF
MARSHALL ISLANDS
PALAU
NAURU
KIRIBATI
TUVALU
TOKELAU

SAMOA

VANUATU
FIJI
COOK IS. (NZ)
NIUE (NZ)
TONGA
NEW CALEDONIA (Fr)
FRENCH POLYNESIA (Fr)

UGANDA
KENYA
RWANDA
BURUNDI
TANZANIA

SOMALIA

MALDIVES

MALAYSIA

SINGAPORE

SEYCHELLES

COMOROS

INDONESIA

PAPUA
NEW
GUINEA

SOLOMON
ISLANDS

ZAMBIA MALAWI
ZIMBABWE

MADAGASCAR

MAURITIUS

TIMOR-LESTE

MOZAMBIQUE

RÉUNION (Fr)

SWAZILAND

LESOTHO

Threatened species are those
assessed as critically endangered,
endangered, or vulnerable by
the International Union for
Conservation of Nature (IUCN).

AUSTRALIA

NEW
ZEALAND

Biodiversity

Biodiversity is the variety between and within species and the different ecosystems in which they (and we) live. Human actions currently threaten more species with global extinction than ever before, and biodiversity is declining faster than at any time in human history.

Not all species have been identified and counted but estimates are that around 1 million species face extinction within decades, unless action is taken to reduce the pace of biodiversity loss. In fact, without countermeasures, the rate of species extinction will accelerate; it is already at least some tens and maybe several hundreds of times higher than the average rate over the past 10 million years.

This loss creates problems for human well-being. Biodiversity is important economically, socially, and medically. An estimated 4 billion people rely primarily on natural medicines for health care. About 70% of drugs used to treat cancer are either natural or are synthetic products that were inspired by natural products. More than 75% of our food crops rely on pollination by insects, birds, and mammals. This includes fruit and vegetables and important cash crops such as coffee, cocoa, and almonds.

Based on satellite data, it has been estimated that there are more trees on Earth than stars in the Milky Way: 3 trillion, or 400 for every living person. But there are fewer now than there used to be. Forests have shrunk by about 20% since 1900 – a loss of 3.9 million square miles (10 million km^2).

Forests matter. More than 2 billion people worldwide rely on burning wood to meet their energy needs. The whole world relies on forests to absorb carbon as part of the planet's natural balance that makes human life possible.

The rate of loss of the world's forests has slowed since 2000; it is 80% less than in the 20th century. But the process is uneven. New planting of temperate and boreal forest in China, USA, and Russia is outweighed by the destruction of highly biodiverse rainforest in Brazil, Indonesia, and the Congo, despite projects regenerating small areas of tropical and subtropical forests.

Unfortunately, for biodiversity, newly planted trees are a poor substitute for mature trees. Better than relying on replacement would be to end the destruction of existing forest land.

Threatened species

Threatened species as percentage of those evaluated by IUCN

2019

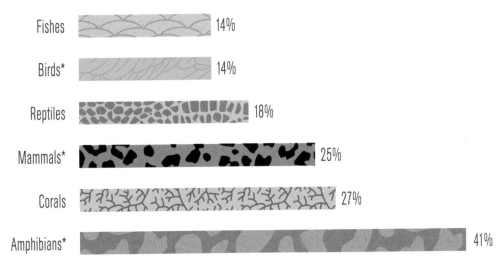

Fishes   14%

Birds*   14%

Reptiles   18%

Mammals*   25%

Corals   27%

Amphibians*   41%

*80% or more of species within group have been evaluated

Forest lost and gained

Top ten most forested countries

2000–2015

square kilometres

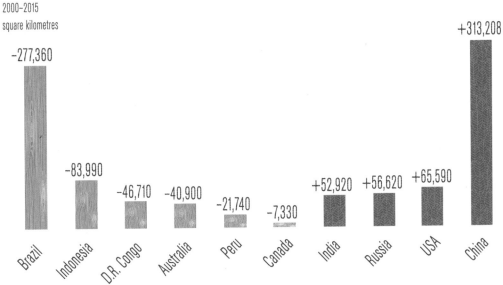

Brazil	Indonesia	D.R. Congo	Australia	Peru	Canada	India	Russia	USA	China
−277,360	−83,990	−46,710	−40,900	−21,740	−7,330	+52,920	+56,620	+65,590	+313,208

Protected areas

Terrestrial protected areas (designated reserves of 1,000 hectares or larger) as percentage of total land area
2018

30% or more
20% – 29%
10% – 19%
less than 10%

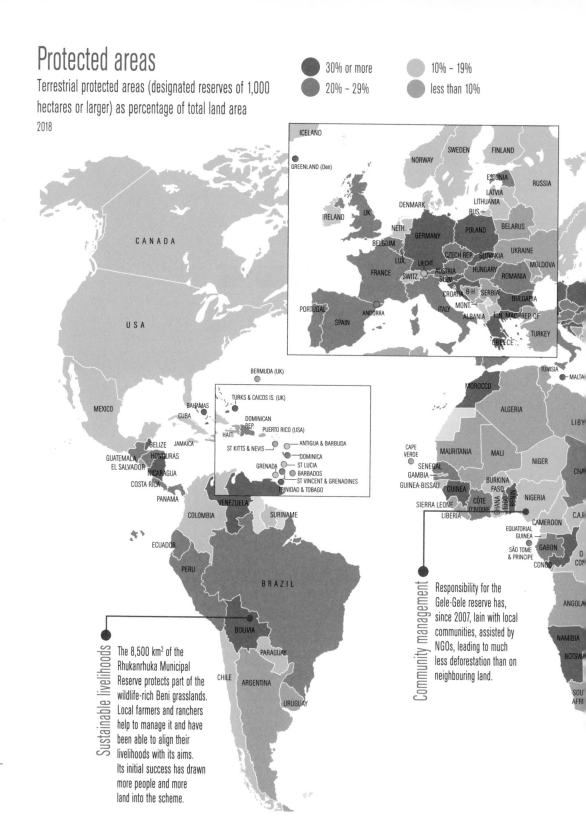

Sustainable livelihoods

The 8,500 km² of the Rhukanrhuka Municipal Reserve protects part of the wildlife-rich Beni grasslands. Local farmers and ranchers help to manage it and have been able to align their livelihoods with its aims. Its initial success has drawn more people and more land into the scheme.

Community management

Responsibility for the Gele-Gele reserve has, since 2007, lain with local communities, assisted by NGOs, leading to much less deforestation than on neighbouring land.

Preservation and public awareness

The Ethiopian wolf, Africa's most endangered carnivore, has benefited from the preservation of its habitat and a reduction in hunting.

Benefits of forest protection

Mainly due to increased forest cover and protection, the population of the endangered Rodrigues fruit bat has recovered from only 70 – 100 individuals in the 1970s to more than 25,000 today.

Water resources

The world as a whole has plenty of fresh water but, like every natural resource, it is distributed unevenly. And, like most natural resources, people are using it at an ever increasing rate. It features in personal use, food production, construction of roads and buildings, and industrial processes, including the manufacture of electronic components.

Freshwater is an unpredictable resource, but is vital for healthy soil and vegetation. When more water is withdrawn than nature resupplies that has an impact on all aspects of the environment: soil, vegetation, the survival of plant and animal species. Countries using more than 25% of their renewable supply are considered by the UN to be water stressed, and those using more than 70% to be seriously stressed.

How the world's water is used:
agriculture: **69%**
industry: **19%**
domestic: **12%**

Increasing water use
Past and projected global water demand
1900–2050
cubic kilometres

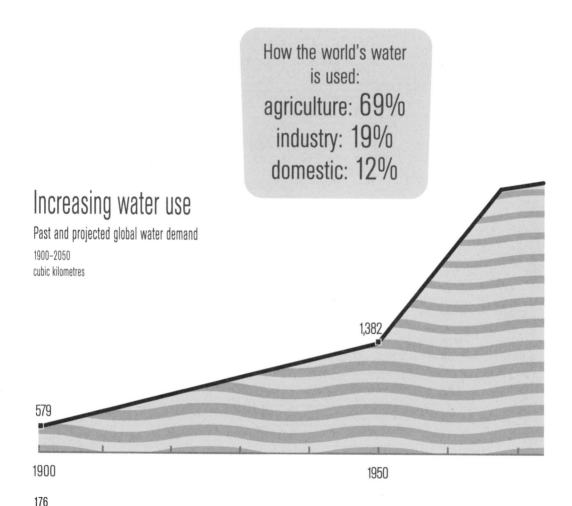

579

1,382

1900

1950

Whether a country has a sufficient, renewable supply of fresh water seems to have little impact on the way of life of its richest inhabitants. Many countries use more water than falls on their territory as rain, flows through it in rivers, or is stored in lakes. In some parts of the world – notably North Africa – water held for millennia in natural underground aquifers is being relentlessly drained. In the Middle East, meagre natural water supplies are supplemented by expensive, energy-consuming desalination plants that have negative effects on the local environment.

Many developed countries compensate for a lack of water by importing food and other goods from countries where water is more plentiful. Others take it a step further. Northern India and areas of China are under severe water stress, which is likely to worsen, and Indian and Chinese investors have purchased large areas of arable land in countries such as Ethiopia, where water supplies are more plentiful.

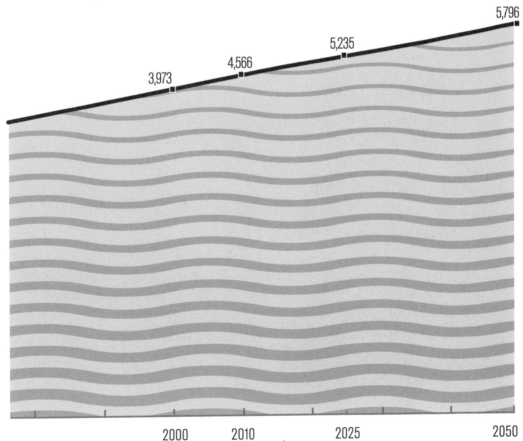

3,973

4,566

5,235

5,796

2000   2010   2025   2050

Water used

Water withdrawn annually per capita for domestic,
industrial, and environmental use

latest available data
2002–2017

cubic metres

- 1,000 – 5,739
- 500 – 999
- 100 – 499
- less than 100
- no data

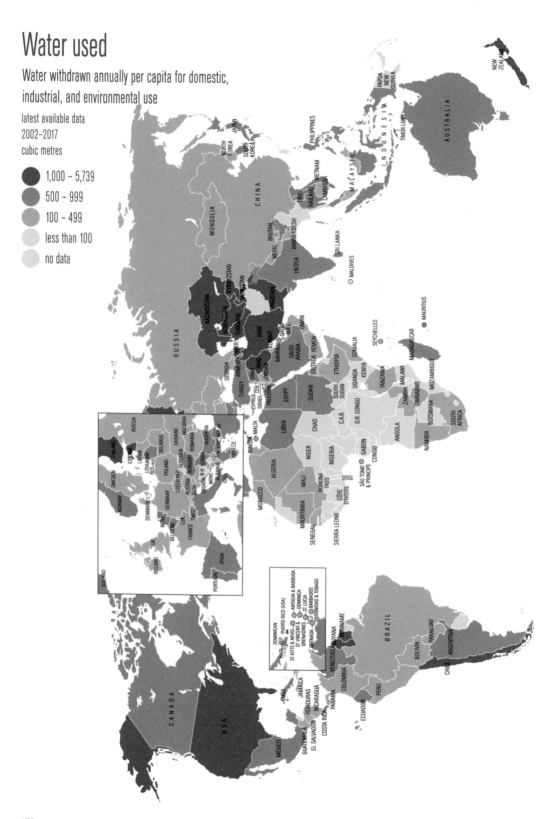

Water stress

Freshwater withdrawal as a percentage
of available resources

latest available data
2002–2017

- 70% or more
  serious water stress
- 25% – 69%
  water stress
- 24% or less
- no data

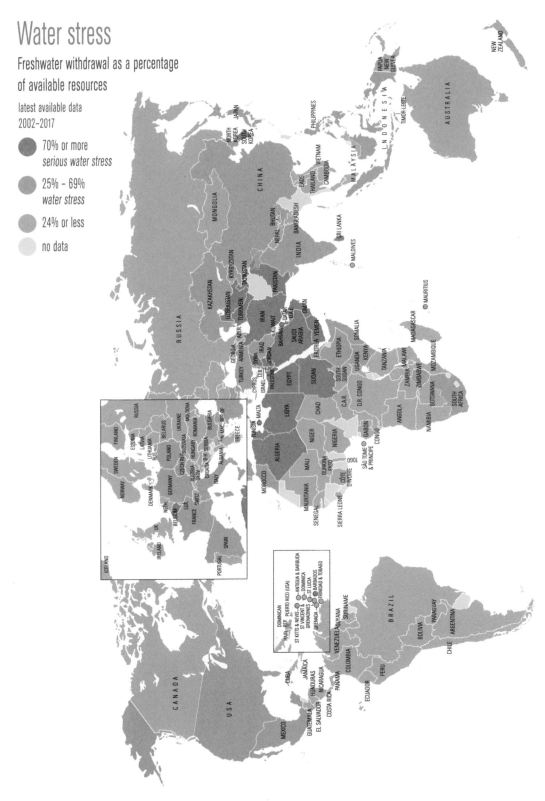

Waste

Waste is one of the world's biggest challenges and, so far, failures. National and local regulations have reduced the use of plastic bags in some countries, but more than half of all waste goes into landfills, often badly managed, and vast areas of ocean are a soup of tiny pieces of plastic.

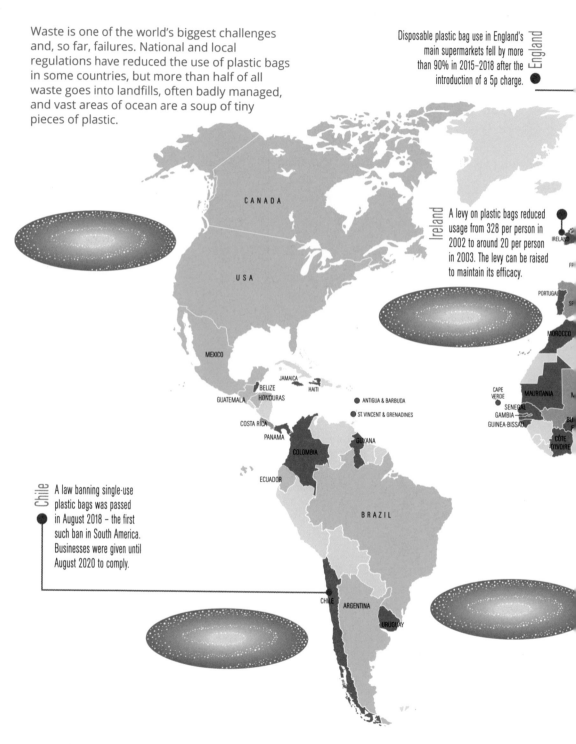

Disposable plastic bag use in England's main supermarkets fell by more than 90% in 2015–2018 after the introduction of a 5p charge. **England**

Ireland A levy on plastic bags reduced usage from 328 per person in 2002 to around 20 per person in 2003. The levy can be raised to maintain its efficacy.

Chile A law banning single-use plastic bags was passed in August 2018 – the first such ban in South America. Businesses were given until August 2020 to comply.

CANADA

USA

MEXICO

JAMAICA

BELIZE
GUATEMALA HONDURAS
HAITI

COSTA RICA
PANAMA

ANTIGUA & BARBUDA
ST. VINCENT & GRENADINES

COLOMBIA

GUYANA

ECUADOR

BRAZIL

CHILE
ARGENTINA

URUGUAY

IRELAND

PORTUGAL

MOROCCO

CAPE VERDE
MAURITANIA
SENEGAL
GAMBIA
GUINEA-BISSAU
CÔTE D'IVOIRE

Plastic waste

Regulations (including ban, levy, or law)
on plastic bags and Styrofoam products
as of 2018

Regulations introduced:
● national
● national regulations announced
● local

○ area where circulating ocean currents cause plastic waste to collect

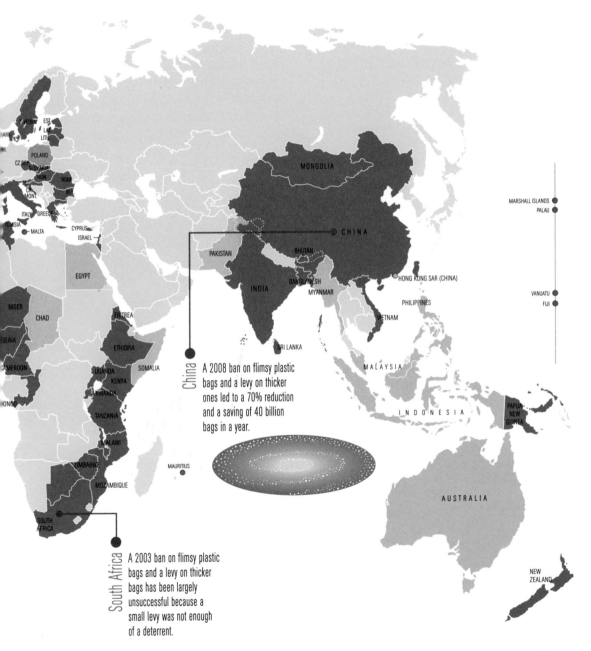

SWEDEN · EST · LA · LITH
POLAND · CZ REP · SLOVAKIA · HUN · ROM · CR · MONT · BUL
ITALY · GREECE
TUNISIA · MALTA · CYPRUS · ISRAEL
EGYPT
NIGER · CHAD · ERITREA
GERIA · ETHIOPIA
AMEROON · UGANDA · KENYA · SOMALIA
ONGO · RWANDA
TANZANIA
MALAWI
ZIMBABWE
MOZAMBIQUE · MAURITIUS
SOUTH AFRICA

PAKISTAN · BHUTAN · BANGLADESH
INDIA · MYANMAR
SRI LANKA
MONGOLIA
CHINA
HONG KONG SAR (CHINA)
PHILIPPINES
VIETNAM
MALAYSIA
INDONESIA
PAPUA NEW GUINEA
AUSTRALIA
NEW ZEALAND

MARSHALL ISLANDS
PALAU
VANUATU
FIJI

China
A 2008 ban on flimsy plastic
bags and a levy on thicker
ones led to a 70% reduction
and a saving of 40 billion
bags in a year.

South Africa
A 2003 ban on flimsy plastic
bags and a levy on thicker
bags has been largely
unsuccessful because a
small levy was not enough
of a deterrent.

181

Waste production

Each year, the world produces about 2 billion tonnes of regular, non-hazardous waste – and this is likely to grow by 70% by 2050 unless urgent action is taken. The USA generates disproportionate amounts: Americans account for only 4% of the world's population, yet generate 12% of its waste.

Only about 16% of global waste is recycled. The US rate of recycling is twice the world average at 35% but well behind the most efficient recycler – Germany – which hits 68%.

It has been estimated that since 1950, the world has produced 8.3 billion tonnes of plastic. Far too much plastic waste has been mishandled and become part of the environment. Most kinds of plastic take from 400 to 1,000 years to degrade. Microplastics – tiny particles of the material – are everywhere, including in our bodies. Their full health and environmental effects are not yet fully known.

By 2050
almost all seabirds
will have
ingested plastic

Plastic world

Global plastic production
million tonnes
1950–2018

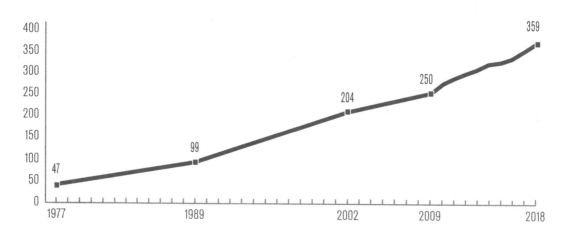

Beach trash

Number of most common items of debris picked up by volunteers
worldwide as Part of Ocean Conservancy clean-up
1985–2018

73m

Plastic bags and
Styrofoam containers
can take up to

1,000 years

to decompose

29m

24m

20m

17m

cigarettes and filters

food wrappers

caps and lids

plastic beverage bottles

plastic bags

Oceans

About 40% of sharks and rays in European waters are threatened with extinction.

Coral reefs Coral reefs cover only 0.1% of the ocean floor but are home to about 25% of marine fish species. The total area of reefs has halved in the past 150 years, increasing pressure on both the animals and people relying on them for nutrition, income, and protection from floods and hurricanes.

North Atlantic right whales Only 300–350 North Atlantic right whales are known to be alive.

Seagrass The area of seagrass has declined by about 30% in the last 100 years. It stabilizes the seabed, provides habitat for marine species, and stores vast amounts of carbon.

Mangroves Important for coastal protection from erosion and storms, as habitat for marine life, and as a CO_2 sink, mangroves have declined by about 30% in the past century.

As of February 2020, 8% of global oceans were classed as protected areas

Ocean dead zones Industrial effluent and climate change has led to at least 500 "dead zones" with very low oxygen levels in coastal waters – a tenfold increase since 1950. Most sea creatures cannot survive in these conditions, but some microbes can. They produce a greenhouse gas that is 300 times more potent than CO_2.

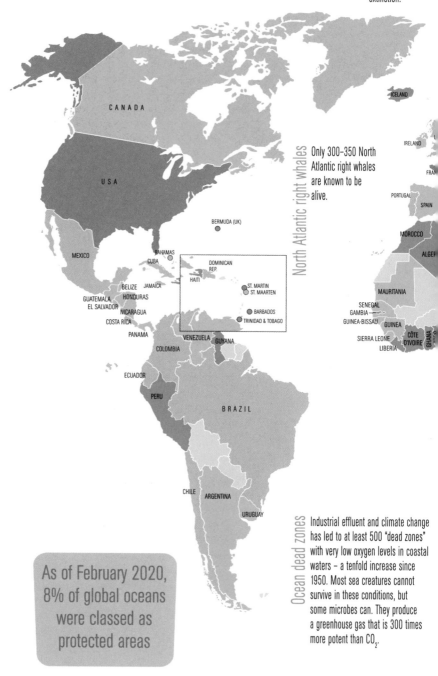

CANADA

USA

MEXICO

BERMUDA (UK)

BAHAMAS

CUBA

BELIZE   JAMAICA
GUATEMALA HONDURAS
EL SALVADOR NICARAGUA
COSTA RICA
PANAMA

HAITI

DOMINICAN REP.

ST. MARTIN
ST. MAARTEN

BARBADOS
TRINIDAD & TOBAGO

VENEZUELA GUYANA
COLOMBIA

ECUADOR

PERU

BRAZIL

CHILE ARGENTINA

URUGUAY

ICELAND

IRELAND

FRAN

PORTUGAL
SPAIN

MOROCCO

ALGER

MAURITANIA

SENEGAL
GAMBIA
GUINEA-BISSAU GUINEA
SIERRA LEONE CÔTE
D'IVOIRE GHANA
LIBERIA

Marine protection

Marine protected area as percentage of
country's territorial waters
2018

83% or more   **11% – 30%**   **local**
31% – 50%   **1% – 10%**   **no access to marine waters, or no data**

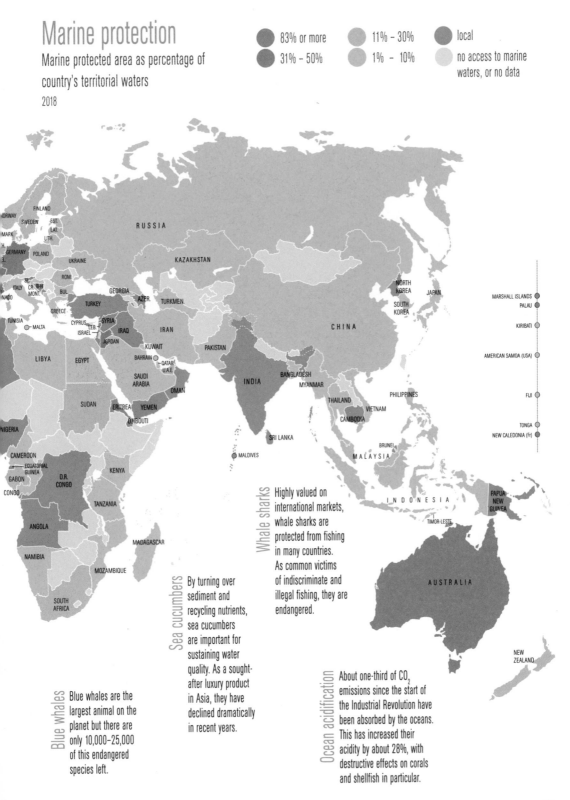

RUSSIA

KAZAKHSTAN

UKRAINE

NORWAY
FINLAND
SWEDEN
EST.
LAT.
MARK.
LITH.
GERMANY
POLAND

ROM.
ITALY
CR. B-H
MONT.
BUL.
GEORGIA
AZER.
TURKMEN.
MONACO
GREECE
TURKEY
TUNISIA
MALTA
CYPRUS
SYRIA
LEB.
ISRAEL
IRAQ
IRAN
JORDAN
KUWAIT
LIBYA
EGYPT
BAHRAIN
QATAR
U.A.E.
SAUDI
ARABIA
OMAN
SUDAN
ERITREA
YEMEN
DJIBOUTI

NORTH
KOREA
SOUTH
KOREA
JAPAN

CHINA

PAKISTAN

INDIA
BANGLADESH
MYANMAR
THAILAND
VIETNAM
CAMBODIA

PHILIPPINES

NIGERIA

CAMEROON
EQUATORIAL
GUINEA
GABON
D.R.
CONGO
CONGO

KENYA

TANZANIA

ANGOLA

NAMIBIA

MOZAMBIQUE

MADAGASCAR

SOUTH
AFRICA

SRI LANKA

MALDIVES

BRUNEI

MALAYSIA

INDONESIA

TIMOR-LESTE

PAPUA
NEW
GUINEA

AUSTRALIA

NEW
ZEALAND

MARSHALL ISLANDS
PALAU
KIRIBATI
AMERICAN SAMOA (USA)
FIJI
TONGA
NEW CALEDONIA (Fr)

Whale sharks Highly valued on
international markets,
whale sharks are
protected from fishing
in many countries.
As common victims
of indiscriminate and
illegal fishing, they are
endangered.

Sea cucumbers By turning over
sediment and
recycling nutrients,
sea cucumbers
are important for
sustaining water
quality. As a sought-
after luxury product
in Asia, they have
declined dramatically
in recent years.

Blue whales Blue whales are the
largest animal on the
planet but there are
only 10,000–25,000
of this endangered
species left.

Ocean acidification About one-third of CO_2
emissions since the start of
the Industrial Revolution have
been absorbed by the oceans.
This has increased their
acidity by about 28%, with
destructive effects on corals
and shellfish in particular.

Energy

Everything that runs, runs on energy. As
countries get richer they use more energy
until a point comes when their economic base
shifts from natural resources and industry to
information and the service sectors.

CANADA

USA

UK

IRELAND

SPAIN

PORTUGAL

MEXICO

MOROCCO ALGERIA

GUATEMALA

CUBA

CÔTE
D'IVOIRE

T. & T.

VENEZUELA

COLOMBIA

ECUADOR

BRAZIL

21% increase

PERU

CHILE

ARGENTINA

Energy use

2015 or latest available data

Total used per year

◯ = 10 million kg of oil equivalent

Use per capita
kg of oil equivalent

- 5,000 or more
- 3,000 – 4,999
- 1,000 – 2,999
- fewer than 1,000

△▽ % change in per capita energy use 2009–2014

NORWAY SWEDEN FINLAND

DEN.

NETHERLANDS

GERMANY POLAND BELARUS

BELGIUM

CZECH REPUBLIC SLOVAKIA

FRANCE

SWITZ. HUNGARY UKRAINE KAZAKHSTAN

AUSTRIA TURKMEN. UZBEKISTAN

ROMANIA

6% decrease

BULGARIA AZER.

ITALY SERBIA TURKEY

GREECE SYRIA IRAQ IRAN

TUNISIA

ISRAEL

KUWAIT

LIBYA BAH.

EGYPT QATAR

SAUDI ARABIA UAE

OMAN

NIGERIA ETHIOPIA

D.R. CONGO KENYA

ANGOLA ZAMBIA TANZANIA

ZIMBABWE

MOZAMBIQUE

SOUTH AFRICA

RUSSIAN FEDERATION
9% increase

NEPAL

PAKISTAN BANGLADESH

INDIA
17% increase

SRI LANKA

NORTH KOREA

SOUTH KOREA
14% increase

CHINA
26% increase

JAPAN
6% decrease

H.K. SAR

VIETNAM

THAILAND PHILIPPINES

MYANMAR MALAYSIA

SINGAPORE INDONESIA

AUSTRALIA

NEW ZEALAND

A changing climate

Melting of the Arctic sea ice over recent decades has reduced its extent and thickness. Heat from the sun is absorbed by the expanded area of open water, possibly creating a feedback loop leading to increased ice melt.

Greenland ice sheet Continued increase in the average global temperature could trigger the irreversible and catastrophic destabilization of the Greenland ice sheet later this century, intensifying a sea-level rise predicted to put about 400 million people at risk of flooding. As the height of the surface ice decreases it is exposed to warmer temperatures at lower altitudes, leading to increased melting.

CANADA
2.1%

USA
24%

World's oceans Absorbing and storing about 40% of CO_2 emissions, the world's oceans are crucial for the global climate. As sea temperatures rise, absorption declines.

Central America & Caribbean
1.6%

SOUTH AMERICA
2.7%

Global emissions of carbon dioxide (CO_2) since 1750 amount to 1.5 trillion tonnes.

Eighty per cent of that total – 1.2 trillion tonnes – has been emitted since 1950, as the use of oil and coal increased sharply in the 1950s and thereafter.

CO_2 makes up 75% of greenhouses gases (GHG). Methane (17%) and nitrous oxide (7%) are the other main GHGs, caused by intensive agriculture. These gases together are warming the atmosphere, with consequences that are unfolding and will intensify.

Amazon rainforest Continuing deforestation will push the Amazon rainforest to a tipping point whereby it loses its ability to renew itself and turns into a source rather than a sink of CO_2. This is expected to occur sometime between 2030 and 2100.

Past emissions and future consequences

Share of total CO_2 emissions from fossil fuels and cement

1950–2014

■ 1% = 12,030 million tonnes CO_2

Permafrost
Areas of permafrost in the northern hemisphere are thawing, releasing stored greenhouse gases into the atmosphere. This increases global warming, which further accelerates the thawing process.

EUROPE
23%

RUSSIA &
CENTRAL ASIA
10%

rest of
EAST ASIA
1.6%

CHINA
14%

JAPAN
4.4%

MIDDLE EAST & NORTH AFRICA
4.8%

SOUTH-EAST ASIA
2.2%

AFRICA
1.9%

SOUTH ASIA
3.5%

3.3%
Other
countries,
plus international
aviation and
shipping

OCEANIA
1.3%

West and East Antarctic ice sheet
The break-up of the West Antarctic ice sheet, a process already begun, could add about 3 m to sea level over the next centuries. Similar processes in the East Antarctic could add an additional 3 – 4 m to sea level.

Impact of increasing emissions

Greenhouse gases continue to build up in the atmosphere. Their impact has already been felt. The world is warmer by an average of 1°C compared to pre-industrial times. That seemingly small change is actually a big difference. Scientists have described the likely effects for at least four decades. These are now unfolding.

In many parts of the world, weather patterns are changing and extreme weather events – prolonged droughts, frequent floods and storms – have become the new norm. Scientific scenarios forecast mostly negative effects on biodiversity and the functioning of ecosystems. Even if global warming is limited to an average of 1.5°C to 2°C, the consequences will be serious.

CO_2 in the atmosphere

Global tropospheric concentration of CO_2
1750–2020
parts per million

 ice-core measurements ▬ atmospheric readings

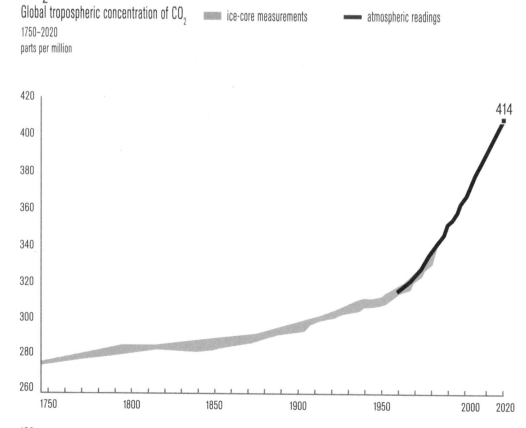

Human cost of natural disasters

As a result of geophysical, meteorological, hydrological, climatological, and extraterrestrial disasters (excluding biological disasters such as insect infestation and diseases)

Total number of people affected:

1990–1999

2000–2009

2010–2019

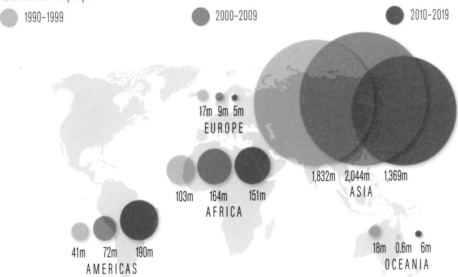

17m 9m 5m
EUROPE

103m 164m 151m
AFRICA

1,832m 2,044m 1,369m
ASIA

41m 72m 190m
AMERICAS

18m 0.6m 6m
OCEANIA

Financial cost of natural disasters

Worldwide

US$

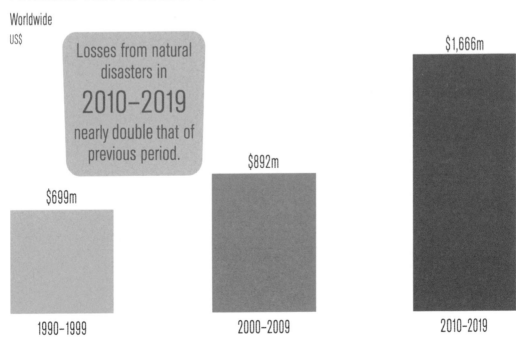

Losses from natural disasters in

2010–2019

nearly double that of previous period.

$699m

$892m

$1,666m

1990–1999

2000–2009

2010–2019

Agreement to change

The 2015 Paris Agreement on climate change established the intention to keep global warming "well below 2°C above pre-industrial levels" and to try to keep it below a 1.5°C rise.

Almost all governments are parties to the Agreement. The USA announced in 2017 that it would withdraw, the only state to do so thus far.

In 2018, the International Governmental Panel on Climate Change (IPCC) set out a timetable of interim targets for reducing greenhouse gas emissions (GHGs).

It also set out the transformations different sectors of the economy will need to make in order to meet these targets.

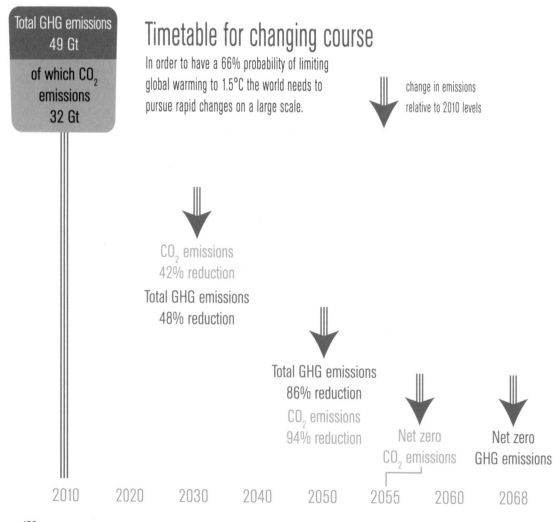

Total GHG emissions
49 Gt

of which CO_2 emissions
32 Gt

Timetable for changing course

In order to have a 66% probability of limiting global warming to 1.5°C the world needs to pursue rapid changes on a large scale.

change in emissions relative to 2010 levels

CO_2 emissions
42% reduction
Total GHG emissions
48% reduction

Total GHG emissions
86% reduction
CO_2 emissions
94% reduction

Net zero
CO_2 emissions

Net zero
GHG emissions

2010 2020 2030 2040 2050 2055 2060 2068

Sectoral changes

Considered necessary by IPCC to achieve 1.5°C goal

Sector	GHG-emitting technologies	Renewables

Energy	Coal as primary energy source:
	    reduce by 75%
	Oil as primary energy source:
	    reduce by 60%
		Non-biomass renewables:
		    increase by 570%
		Energy-related investment:
		    US$830 billion more a year

Power	Coal-fired power:
	    reduce by 70% by 2030
	    reduce by 100% by 2050
		Renewables as share of electricity generation
		    increase by 75%+

Transport	Oil consumption:
	    reduce by 25% – 75% through electrification,
	    greater use of public transport, bicycles and
	    walking
		Low-emission final energy:
		    increase to 35% – 65% share in transport

Industry	CO_2 emissions:
	    reduce by 65% – 90% through increased
	    efficiency, electrification, substitution of
	    carbon-intensive products, and use of carbon
	    capture and storage methods	

Building	Electricity as share of energy used in buildings:
	    reduce by 55% – 75%
		Energy use intensity of buildings:
		    improve through modernization, behavioural
		    change, and increased efficiency of heating/
		    ventilation-systems.

Land-use	Reforms:
	    reduction to net zero land-use emissions by
	    2025–2040 and negative emissions by 2050
	    reduction in non-CO_2 emissions in agricultural
	    sector
	    reduction in food waste
	    reduction in meat consumption
		Means to reach these goals:
		    increase in re/afforestation
		    increase in restoration and conservation of
		    natural ecosystems
		    improvement in management of resources
		    increased use of bioenergy, carbon capture,
		    and storage mechanisms

A greening world

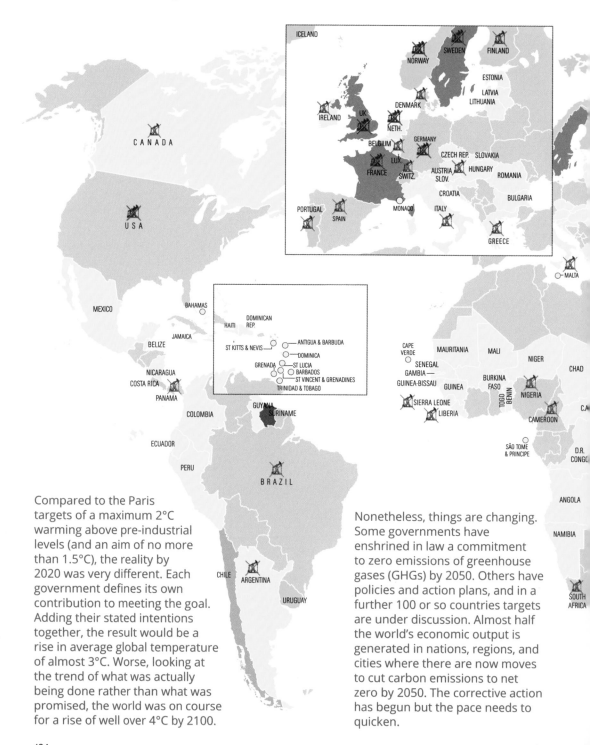

Compared to the Paris targets of a maximum 2°C warming above pre-industrial levels (and an aim of no more than 1.5°C), the reality by 2020 was very different. Each government defines its own contribution to meeting the goal. Adding their stated intentions together, the result would be a rise in average global temperature of almost 3°C. Worse, looking at the trend of what was actually being done rather than what was promised, the world was on course for a rise of well over 4°C by 2100.

Nonetheless, things are changing. Some governments have enshrined in law a commitment to zero emissions of greenhouse gases (GHGs) by 2050. Others have policies and action plans, and in a further 100 or so countries targets are under discussion. Almost half the world's economic output is generated in nations, regions, and cities where there are now moves to cut carbon emissions to net zero by 2050. The corrective action has begun but the pace needs to quicken.

Commitment to net zero emissions

Countries' legislative plans to achieve net zero emissions
of GHGs by 2050 at the latest

as of March 2020

- already achieved
- set in national legislation
- proposed for national legislation
- proposed in policy document
- target under discussion
- no commitment or no data

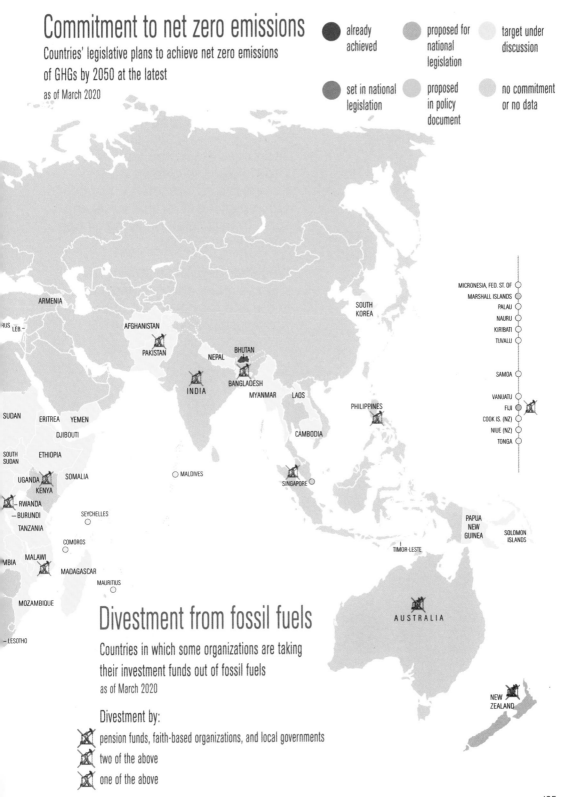

MICRONESIA, FED. ST. OF
MARSHALL ISLANDS
PALAU
NAURU
KIRIBATI
TUVALU

SAMOA

VANUATU
FIJI
COOK IS. (NZ)
NIUE (NZ)
TONGA

ARMENIA

AFGHANISTAN

PAKISTAN

NEPAL

BHUTAN

BANGLADESH

INDIA

MYANMAR

LAOS

SOUTH KOREA

PHILIPPINES

CAMBODIA

SUDAN   ERITREA   YEMEN

DJIBOUTI

SOUTH SUDAN   ETHIOPIA

UGANDA   SOMALIA
KENYA

RWANDA
BURUNDI
TANZANIA

MALDIVES

SINGAPORE

SEYCHELLES

COMOROS

MBIA   MALAWI

MADAGASCAR

MAURITIUS

MOZAMBIQUE

LESOTHO

CYRUS   LEB.

PAPUA NEW GUINEA

SOLOMON ISLANDS

TIMOR-LESTE

AUSTRALIA

NEW ZEALAND

Divestment from fossil fuels

Countries in which some organizations are taking
their investment funds out of fossil fuels

as of March 2020

Divestment by:

- pension funds, faith-based organizations, and local governments
- two of the above
- one of the above

195

Finding alternatives

The climate-change risks of continuing to emit carbon from fossil fuels have led to interest and investment in alternatives.

Because each has benefits and drawbacks, the lobbies for and against have cogent arguments. Nuclear power can look good from a climate perspective, less so when viewed through the lens of hazardous waste.

Biofuels seem environmentally responsible, but producing them takes so much energy it is not clear how big the gain is, and they also take land out of food production. The wind, waves, tide, and sun are all sources of unending energy. Technologies to convert these natural forces into energy and heat are improving at a rapid pace, and solar, in particular, is seeing a huge increase in capacity.

Whatever differences these energy sources make, the key alternative in the end may well turn out to be simply using less.

Growth in renewables

Average annual growth rate of renewables capacity and biofuels production
2009–2018
2011–2018*
2013–2018**

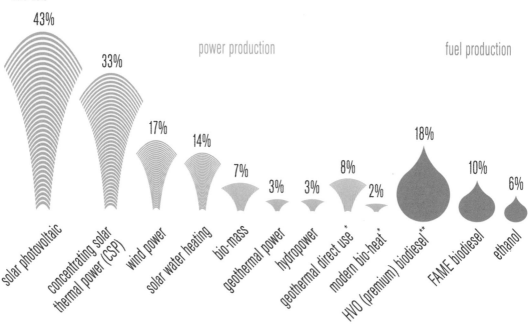

power production   fuel production

- 43% solar photovoltaic
- 33% concentrating solar thermal power (CSP)
- 17% wind power
- 14% solar water heating
- 7% bio-mass
- 3% geothermal power
- 3% hydropower
- 8% geothermal direct use *
- 2% modern bio-heat *
- 18% HVO (premium) biodiesel**
- 10% FAME biodiesel
- 6% ethanol

Green initiatives

Trees and plants absorb carbon dioxide, and 11% of global emissions of greenhouse gases (GHGs) are caused by the destruction of forests. Much work has been done over recent decades to try and reduce deforestation, most recently through schemes that provide local people with economic incentives and opportunities linked to the protection or restoration of forested areas.

In the Sahel region of Africa, a scheme was launched in 2007 to restore degraded lands that are being encroached on by the desert. The aim is that by 2030 a Great Green Wall, consisting of 100 million hectares of restored land, will stretch 5,000 miles (8,000 km) across the continent. As well as bringing environmental benefits, it will improve the economy and food security of the communities in the region, and provide millions of jobs for the people living along it.

The Great Green Wall

as of March 2020

Senegal — 12m drought-resistant trees planted in less than a decade

Niger — 5m hectares of restored land produces enough grain to feed 2.5m people

Ethiopia — 15m hectares of degraded land restored

Sources

WHO WE ARE

United Nations Department of Economic and Social Affairs (DESA), Population Division. World Population Prospects 2019. Retr'd 17 June 2019, population.un.org/wpp

King R. The atlas of human migration. London: Earthscan, 2010.

14–17 States of the world

Sovereignty
Heath-Brown N. The statesman's yearbook – The politics, cultures and economies of the world. London: Palgrave Macmillan; 2019.

CIA. The World Factbook. Retr'd 17 June 2019, www.cia.gov

State formation
Encyclopedia Britannica. Retr'd 1 Oct 2019, www.britannica.com

BBC. BBC Country Profiles. Retr'd 27 Sept 2019, www.bbc.com

Heath-Brown N. op cit.

CIA. The World Factbook. Retr'd 17 June 2019, www.cia.gov

18–19 Population
World Demographics. Retr'd 17 June 2019, www.worldometers

People in the world
UN DESA, Population Division. World Population Prospects 2019. Retr'd 17 June 2019, population.un.org/wpp

Changing population
UN DESA, Population Division. The world at six billion. Author; 1999.

UN DESA; 2019, op cit.

20–21 Life expectancy

Life expectancy at birth
WHO. Global Health Observatory Data Repository. Life expectancy and healthy life expectancy. Retr'd 17 June 2019, www.who.int

CIA. The World Factbook. Retr'd 17 June 2019, www.cia.gov

Living longer
Riley JC. Estimates of regional and global life expectancy, 1800–2001. Population and Development Review. 2005;31(3):537-543.

WHO, op cit.

22–23 Women and men

Women in the world
World Bank. World Development Indicators. Retr'd 19 June 2019, www.data.worldbank.org

CIA. The World Factbook: Sex ratio. Retr'd 17 June 2019, www.cia.gov

Baby boys and girls
World Bank, op cit.

China Statistical Yearbook 2018. Beijing: China Statistics Press; 2019. stats.gov.cn

24–27 Ethnicity and diversity

Ethnic, national, and racial minorities
Minority Rights Group. World directory of minorities and indigenous peoples. 2019. Retr'd 31 July 2019, www.minorityrights.org

CIA. The World Factbook. Retr'd 31 July 2019, www.cia.gov

Migrants
United Nations Department of Economic and Social Affairs (DESA), Population Division. Trends in international migrant stock: The 2017 revision.

China Statistical Yearbook 2018. Beijing: China Statistics Press; 2019. stats.gov.cn

The language of government
CIA. op cit.

Holmes O, Balousha, H. One more racist law: Reactions as Israel axes Arabic as official language. The Guardian, 19 July 2018. www.theguardian.com

28–31 Religious beliefs

Believers
CIA. The World Factbook. Retr'd 19 June 2019, www.cia.gov

Hackett C et al. Global Christianity: A report on the size and distribution of the world's Christian population. Washington, DC: Pew Research Centre; 2011.

Miller T. Mapping the global Muslim population: A report on the size and distribution of the world's Muslim population. Washington, DC: Pew Research Center; 2009.

PEW Research Center. PEW-Templeton Global Religious Futures Project. Retr'd 20 June 2019, www.globalreligiousfutures.org

Kosovo: Mughal AG. Muslims in Kosovo: A socio-economic and demographic profile: Is the Muslim population exploding? Balkan Social Science Review. 2015;6:155-201.

Oman: Who are the Ibadis?

The Economist. 18 Dec 2018. www.economist.com

World faiths
Grim, BJ, et al. Yearbook of international religious demography 2018. Brill; 2018.

Hackett, op cit.

Miller, op cit.

Non-believers
Hackett, op cit.

32–35 Literacy and education

Adult illiteracy
UNESCO Institute for Statistics. Literacy rate, adult total. Retr'd 20 June 2019, www.data.uis.unesco.org

Primary education • Secondary education • Tertiary education
World Bank. World Development Indicators. Retr'd 19 June 2019, www.data.worldbank.org

36–39 Urbanization
UN DESA. 68% of the world population projected to live in urban areas by 2050, says UN. 16 May 2018. Retr'd 12 Dec 2019, www.un.org

Urban population
UN DESA, Population Division. World Population Prospects 2019. Retr'd 19 June 2019, population.un.org

World Bank. World Development Indicators 2019. Retr'd 19 June 2019, www.data.worldbank.org

Global urban population • Ten largest cities • City scale
UN DESA. World Urbanization Prospects 2018. New York: United Nations, 2018, population.un.org. Retr'd 26 May 2020.

WEALTH AND POVERTY

42–43 Income

Gross National Income • Economic growth
World Bank. World Development Indicators. Retr'd 19 June 2019, www.data.worldbank.org

44–47 Inequality

Distribution of wealth
World Bank. World Development Indicators. Retr'd 19 June 2019, www.data.worldbank.org

Gender pay gap
International Labour Organization. Global wage report 2018/19: What lies behind gender pay gaps? Geneva: ILO; 2018.

World poverty

CIA. The World Factbook. Retr'd 23 Oct 2019, www.cia.gov

World Bank, op cit.

The hands of a few

Kroll L. Billionaires – The richest people in the world: Mapping the world's richest. 2019. Retr'd 25 June 2019, www.forbes.com

Bouncing back

Kroll L, Miller M, Serafin T. The world's billionaires. Forbes; 2009.

Kroll, op cit.

48–49 Quality of Life

Relative human development • Wealth for wellbeing?

United Nations Development Programme (UNDP). Human Development Indices and Indicators – 2018 Statistical Update. New York: Author; 2018.

50–51 Transnationals

Corporate wealth exceeds country wealth

Fortune. Global 500. Retr'd 28 June 2019, www.fortune.com

World Bank. World Development Indicators. Retr'd 23 July 2019, www.data.worldbank.org

Winners and losers

Dehua C. Fortune Global 500 rankings sees China closing gap on US. Retr'd July 23 2019, www.gbtimes.com

Global 500, 2017.

Global 500, 2018.

52–53 Banks

Comparative wealth • Weighed in the balance

Fortune. Global 500. Retr'd 28 June 2019, www.fortune.com

World Bank. World Development Indicators. Retr'd 23 July 2019, www.data.worldbank.org

54–59 Corruption

Rate of corruption

Transparency International. Corruption Perceptions Index 2018. Retr'd 28 June 2019, www.transparency.org

Shadow economy

Schneider LMF. Shadow economies around the world: What did we learn over the last 20 years? IMF Working Paper. Washington, DC: International Monetary Fund (IMF); 2018.

Panama and Paradise Papers

Bullough O. Moneyland. London: Profile; 2018.

Obermaier F, Wormer V, Jaschensky W. About the Panama Papers. Retr'd 20 Sept 2019, www.panamapapers.sueddeutsche.de

Obermayer B, Obermaier F. The Panama Papers. London: Oneworld; 2016.

Offshore financial services

International Consortium of Investigative Journalists (ICIJ). Explore the Panama Papers key figures. 2017. Retr'd 20 Sept 2019, www.icij.org

Panama and Paradise • power players

ICIJ. The power players. Retr'd 20 Sept 2019, www.icij.org

Panama Papers • effects of leak

Shabbir, LGN. Gauging the global impacts of the Panama Papers three years later. Reuters Institute for the Study of Journalism; 2019.

60–61 Debt

Global debt edged up in 2018, debt ratio little changed: IIF. Reuters. Business News. 2 Apr 2019. www.reuters.com

Government debt

International Monetary Fund (IMF). General government gross debt (Percentage of GDP). Retr'd 1 July 2019, www.imf.org

Household debt

IMF. Private debt, loans and debt securities (percent of GDP). 2019. Retr'd 1 July 2019, www.imf.org

Total household debt

Samuelson RJ. With booming global debt we're entering unexplored territory. The Washington Post. 16 Jan 2019.

62–63 How the money's made

Which sector dominates a country's economy?

The World Bank. World Development Indicators: Structure of output. Retr'd 24 July 2019, www.wdi.worldbank.org

Tourism dependency

World Travel & Tourism Council. Total contribution to GDP. Retr'd 2 July 2019, www.wttc.org

RIGHTS AND RESPECT

65–69 Political systems

Current political systems

Freedom House. Freedom in the world 2018 – Country reports. Retr'd 17 July 2019, www.freedomhouse.org

Heath-Brown N. The statesman's yearbook – The politics, cultures and economies of the world. London: Palgrave Macmillan; 2019.

Congo, Dem Rep: Doss A, Ibrahim M. Congo's Election: A defeat for democracy, a disaster for the people. 9 Feb 2019. Retr'd 18 July 2019, www.theguardian.com

Libya: BBC News. Libya country profile. Retr'd 18 July 2019, www.bbc.com

Mauritania: Thomas-Johnson A. Mauritanian authorities brutally crack down on post-election protests, videos show. 2019. Retr'd 22 July 2019, www.middleeasteye.net

South Sudan: UN News. South Sudan's peace process precarious, but progress is being made, Security Council hears. 2019. Retr'd 24 Oct 2019, www.news.un.org

Living politics

UN DESA, Population Division. World Population Prospects 2019, Online Edition.

Transition to and from democracy

Heath-Brown N. The statesman's yearbook – The politics, cultures and economies of the world. London: Palgrave Macmillan; 2019.

Albania and Colombia: CIA. The World Factbook. Retr'd 16 July 2019, www.cia.gov

Algeria, Bhutan, Chad, Republic of Congo, Denmark, Egypt, El Salvador, Japan, Kyrgyzstan, Lebanon, Mozambique, South Sudan, Tonga, Tunisia, United Kingdom: BBC News. Country Profiles. www.bbc.co.uk

Cameroon, Dominica, Liberia, Libya, Moldova, Tanzania: Encyclopedia Britannica. Country profiles. Retr'd 27 Nov 2019, www.britannica.com

New Zealand: Teara. The encyclopedia of New Zealand. teara.govt.nz

Trinidad & Tobago, Uganda: Freedom House. Freedom in the world 2018 – Country reports. www.freedomhouse.org

70–71 Religious rights

State attitude towards religion

Pew Research Center. Many countries favor specific religions, officially or unofficially. 3 Oct 2017.

US Department of State. 2018 Report on international religious freedom. www.state.gov

China: CIA. The World Factbook: China. Retr'd 23 Oct 2019, www.cia.gov

North Korea/Vietnam: United States Commission on International Religious Freedom (USCIRF). 2019 annual report. Washington, DC; 2019.

Samoa: Wyeth G. Samoa officially becomes a Christian state. 2017. www.thediplomat.com

Islamic law

CIA. The World Factbook: Legal System. Retr'd 23 Oct 2019, www.cia.gov

Hauser Global Law School Program, New York University School of Law, 2019. GlobaLex. Retr'd 23 Oct 2019, www.nyulawglobal.org

Heath-Brown N. The statesman's yearbook – The politics, cultures and economies of the world. London: Palgrave Macmillan; 2019.

US Department of State. 2018 Report on International Religious Freedom, 2019. Retr'd 23 Oct 2019, www.state.gov

72–77 Human rights

Extreme abuses of human rights

Amnesty International. Amnesty International report 2017/18 – The state of the world's human rights. 2018.

Human Rights Watch. World report 2019 – Events of 2018 USA. 2019.

US Department of State. 2018 Country reports on human rights practices. 2019.

Judicial killings

Amnesty International, op cit.

Death Penalty Information Center. Retr'd 21 Oct 2019, www.deathpenaltyinfo.org

Sex trafficking

United Nations Office on Drugs and Crime (UNODC). Global report on trafficking in persons 2018: Country profiles. Vienna; 2018.

Cambodia: US Department of State. 2017, p.25.

France: US Department of State. Trafficking in persons report 2016, p.12.

Honduras to USA, Romania to

Germany: US Department of State. Trafficking in persons report 2019, p.13.

Nigeria to Italy: US Department of State. Trafficking in persons report 2018, op. cit. p.8.

Syria to Lebanon: US Department of State. Trafficking in persons report 2017, p.4.

USA: US Department of State. op cit, 2018, p.10.

Child abuse

Swarens T. How many people are victims of sex trafficking? IndyStar. 14 Dec 2019. eu.indystar.com

78–81 Children's rights

Unregistered children

UNICEF Global Databases. Birth registration. Retr'd 16 Oct 2019, www.data.unicef.org

Children at work • Children at risk

International Labour Organization (ILO). Methodology: Global estimates of child labour, 2012–2016. Geneva: Author; 2017, pp.96–98.

Children not in school

The World Bank. Education statistics. Retr'd 15 Nov 2019, www.databank.worldbank.org

82–85 Women's rights

Equal rights • Change in gender inequality

United Nations Development Programme (UNDP). Human Development Reports Data (1990–2017): Gender Inequality Index (GII). Retr'd 7 July 2019, www.hdr.undp.org

Women in parliament

UNDP. Human Development Reports Data (1990–2017): Share of seats in parliament (% held by women). Retr'd 7 July 2019, www.hdr.undp.org

Powerful women

Wikipedia. List of elected and appointed female heads of state and government. Retr'd 25 Nov 2019, www.wikipedia.org

86–89 LGBTQ rights

Legal status

Mendos LR. State-sponsored homophobia 2019. Geneva: International Lesbian, Gay, Bisexual, Trans and Intersex-Association; 2019.

Greenland, Taiwan: Pew Research Center (PEW). Same-sex marriage around the world. Retr'd 12 Nov 2019, www.pewforum.org

The right to adopt

Mendos, op cit.

The right to serve

Polchar J, Sweijs T, Marten P, Galdiga JH. LGBT Military Index 2014. The Hague: The Hague Centre for Strategic Studies; 2014.

90–91 Minorities

Peoples under threat

Minority Rights Group. Peoples under threat 2019. Retr'd 24 Oct 2019, www.peoplesunderthreat.org

92–93 Freedom

Freedom in the world • Changing times

Freedom House. Freedom in the World Countries. Retr'd 17 July 2019, www.freedomhouse.org

WAR AND PEACE

96–99 Wars this century

At war

Raleigh C, Linke A, Hegre H, Karlsen J. Introducing ACLED-Armed Conflict Location and Event Data. Journal of Peace Research. 2010;47(5):651-660. Retr'd 2 Nov 2019, www.acleddata.com

Chad: Pujol-Mazzini A. Suicide bomber kills five in Chad, including soldier. 12 Oct 2019. Retr'd 18 Nov 2019, www.reuters.com

Israel: Morris L, Eglash R, Balousha H. Death toll rises as Gaza militants fire hundreds of rockets into Israel, which responds with airstrikes. Washington Post, 5 May 2019. www.washingtonpost.com

Kenya: Bomb kills Kenyan police near Somali border. The Guardian, 13 Oct 2019. www.theguardian.com

Kenya: Torchia C. Death toll in Nairobi attack climbs to 21, plus 5 attackers. 2019. Retr'd 18 Nov 2019, www.apnews.com

Mozambique: Helms E. Regional overview: Africa. 27 Oct – 2 Nov 2019. The Armed Conflict Location & Event Data Project (ACLED).

Nigeria: BBC News. Dozens of mourners killed by Boko Haram at a funeral in north Nigeria. 28 July 2019. www.bbc.com

Rwanda: Helms E, Karacalti A. Regional overview: Africa. 6 – 12 Oct 2019. The Armed Conflict Location & Event Data Project (ACLED).

Uganda: Nantulya P. Ever-adaptive allied democratic forces insurgency. 2019. Retr'd 18 Nov 2019, www.africacenter.org

Rising tensions

Gleditsch NP et al. Armed Conflict 1946–2001: A new dataset. Journal of Peace Research. 2002;39(5):615-637.

Pettersson T, Högbladh S, Öberg M. Organized Violence, 1989–2018 and peace agreements. Journal of Peace Research. 2019;56(4).

Pettersson T. UCDP/PRIO Armed Conflict Dataset Codebook v 19.1.

Uppsala Conflict Data Program (UCDP) www.ucdp.uu.se

Uppsala Conflict Data Program (UCDP) www.ucdp.uu.se

Fighting outside borders

Aspa JMR, Rufanges JC. Democratic Republic of Congo: A review of 20 years of war. Centre Delàs d'Estudis per la Pau/Escola de Cultura de Pau; 2016.

Gleditsch et al, 2002, op cit.

Pettersson et al, 2019, op cit.

Pettersson, 2019, op cit.

100–103 Warlords, ganglords, and militias

Non-state armed forces

Aboudi, S. In Yemen chaos, Islamic State grows to rival al Qaeda. Reuters, 30 June 2015. www.reuters.com

Al Jazeera. Saudi-UAE coalition cut deals with al-Qaeda in Yemen. Al Jazeera, 6 Aug 2018. www.aljazeera.com

Allister EM. Gunmen kill 13 in Senegal's Casamance region: Army. Reuters, 6 Jan 2018 www.reuters.com

BBC News. IS caliphate defeated but jihadist group remains a threat. BBC News, 23 Mar 2019. www.bbc.com

Behera A, Sharma SK. Militant groups in South Asia. Institute for Defence Studies and Analyses. New Delhi: Pentagon Press; 2014.

Bhaumik S. Myanmar has a new insurgency to worry about. This Week in Asia, 1 Sept 2017. www.scmp.com

Blanford N, Spyer J. Israel raises alarm over advances by Hizbullah and Iran. Jane's Military & Security Assessments Intelligence Centre; 2017.

Brady T. Threat level remains severe after merger of terror groups. Irish Independent, 14 Sept 2012. www.independent.ie

Browning N, Sharafedin B. In Iran, Islamic State seeks to fan militancy among minorities. Reuters, 15 Aug 2017. www.reuters.com

Casey N. Colombia's peace deal promised a new era. So why are these rebels rearming? The New York Times, 17 May 2019. www.nytimes.com

Center for Strategic and International Studies. Backgrounder: Islamic State Khorasan (IS-K). 2018.

Chang I-W, Haiyun Ma J. For them, Afghanistan is safer than China. Foreign Policy, 1 Nov 2018. www.foreignpolicy.com

Congo Research Group, New York University's Center on International Cooperation & Human Rights Watch (2019). KIVU Security Tracker: Armed groups. Retr'd 20 Nov 2019, www.kivusecurity.org

Cube C. The Taliban is gaining strength and territory in Afghanistan. NBC News, 30 Jan 2018. www.nbcnews.com

Dukhan, N. Splintered warfare: Alliances, affiliations, and agendas of armed factions and politico-military groups in the Central African Republic. Enough Project: 2017. enoughproject.org

Ebbighausen R. Southeast Asia in the crosshairs of Islamic State. 15 Oct 2019. www.dw.com

Heinrich M, Lewis A. Forces under Libya's Haftar say they're close to taking final eastern holdout. Reuters (online), 14 June 2018. www.af.reuters.com

Immigration and Refugee Board of Canada (2016). Brazil: First Command of the Capital (Primeiro Comando da Capital, PCC), including activities, targets, group structure and areas of operation; state protection for victims and witnesses of PCC crimes (2012 – Mar 2016). Ottawa.

Immigration and Refugee Board of Canada (2019). Brazil: The Red Command (Comando Vermelho, CV) criminal organization, including activities, areas of operation, membership, structure, networks, political connections, and resources; state protection available for victims of crimes committed by the Red Command (2017–Mar 2019). Ottawa.

International Crisis Group. Q&A: Boko Haram in Cameroon: Interview with Hans de Marie Heungoup.

2016. Retr'd 25 Nov 2019, www.crisisgroup.org

Jason Warner J, Hulme C. The Islamic State in Africa: Estimating fighter numbers in cells across the continent. CTC Sentinel. 2018;11(7):21-27.

Knights M. The JRTN Movement and Iraq's next insurgency. CTC Sentinel. 2011;4(7):1-6.

Lister C. Al Qaeda is starting to swallow the Syrian opposition. Foreign Policy, 15 Mar 2017. www.foreignpolicy.com

Martin P, Piccolino G, Speight J. Rebel networks' deep roots cause concerns for Côte d'Ivoire transition. Global Observatory, International Peace Institute; 2017. Retr'd 25 Nov 2019, www.theglobalobservatory.org

Morris L. Is China backing Indian insurgents? The Diplomat. 22 Mar 2011. www.thediplomat.com

Nayak D K. Naxal violence: The Peoples' Liberation Front of India (PLFI) in Jharkhand. Institute of Peace and Conflict Studies (IPCS); 29 Mar 2013. www.ipcs.org

Neuhof F. Iran's forgotten Kurds step up the struggle. The National, 16 Apr 2016. www.thenational.ae.

Pack J. Kingdom of militias: Libya's second war of post-Qadhafi succession, Italian Institute for International Political Studies (ISPI); 2019.

Reuters. Search for PJAK in 2019.

Sánchez MIC. Paramilitarism and state-terrorism in mexico as a case study of shrinking functions of the neoliberal state. Perspectives on Global Development and Technology. 2014;13:176-196.

Shih, G. AP Exclusive: Uighurs fighting in Syria take aim at China. AP News, 27 Dec 2017. www.apnews.com

South Asia Terrorism Portal (SATP), Institute of Conflict Management (ICM). India - Terrorists, Insurgents and extremist groups. 2017. Retr'd 21 Nov 2019, www.satp.org

Stanford University, Center for International Security and Cooperation (CISAC), SU. Mapping militants. 2018. www.cisac.fsi.stanford.edu

The Economic Times. Government bans militant outfit NSCN(K) for five years. 14 July 2018. economictimes.indiatimes.com

United Nations Security Council (2018). Final report of the Group of Experts on the Democratic Republic of the Congo S/2018/531.

United Nations Security Council (2018). Jemmah Anshorut Tauhid (JAT). Update as of 17 July 2018. www.un.org

Uppsala University, Department of Peace and Conflict Research, Uppsala Conflict Data Program. Retr'd 21 Nov 2019, www.ucdp.uu.se

US Department of Defense, US Department of State, US Agency for International Development (2019). Operation Freedom's Sentinel. Lead Inspector General Report to the United States Congress, 1 Jan 2019 – 31 Mar 2019.

Armed conflict

Pettersson T, Högbladh S, Öberg M. Organized violence, 1989-2018 and peace agreements. Journal of Peace Research. 2019;56(4).

Pettersson T. UCDP Non-state conflict codebook v 19.1. Uppsala Conflict Data Program, Department of Peace and Conflict Research Uppsala University; 2019.

Sundberg R, Eck K, Kreutz J. Introducing the UCDP Non-State Conflict Dataset. Journal of Peace Research, 2012;49(2):351-362.

Children at war

Nations General Assembly Security Council (2019). Children and armed conflict: Report of the Secretary-General A/73/907-S/2019/509.

104–07 Military muscle

Military spending • Top military spenders

Stockholm International Peace Research Institute (SIPRI). SIPRI Military Expenditure Database. Stockholm 2020.

Armed forces top ten

International comparisons of defence expenditure and military personnel. The Military Balance. 2020;120(1): 529-534.

108–111 Mass destruction

Declining stockpiles • Nuclear warhead stockpiles

Natural Resources Defense Council. Global nuclear stockpiles, 1945-2006. Bulletin of the Atomic Scientists. 2006;62(4):64-66.

Stockholm International Peace Research Institute (SIPRI). SIPRI yearbook. Oxford, UK: Oxford University Press. 2000-2019.

Nuclear accidents

atomicarchive.com (2015). Broken arrows: Nuclear weapons accidents. www.atomicarchive.com

Edwards A, Gregory S. The hidden cost of deterrence: Nuclear weapons accidents 1950–88. Bulletin of Peace Proposals 1989;20(1):3-26.

Hansen C. The swords of Armageddon. v2. vol VII. The development of US nuclear weapons (CD-ROM version), Chukelea Publications; 2007.

Petersen B. The atomic bomb that faded into South Carolina history. Military Times. 31 Mar 2018. www.militarytimes.com

US Department of Defense. Narrative summaries of accidents involving US nuclear weapons 1950–1980.

Chemical weapons in Syria

Sanders-Zakre A. Timeline of Syrian chemical weapons activity, 2012–2019. Arms Control Association; 2019. Retr'd 25 Nov 2019, www.armscontrol.org

Chemical attacks in Syria

Lütkefend T, Schneider T. Nowhere to hide. The logic of chemical weapons use in Syria. Global Public Policy Institute (GPPi); 2019.

112–115 Casualties of War

Death toll this century • Regional toll • Type of conflict

Iraq Body Count. Documented civilian deaths from violence from 2003–2019. Retr'd 2 Dec 2019, www.iraqbodycount.org

Raleigh C, Linke A, Hegre A, Karlsen J. Introducing ACLED-Armed Conflict Location and Event Data. Journal of Peace Research. 2010;47(5):651-660.

Ralph S, Melander E. Introducing the UCDP georeferenced event dataset. Journal of Peace Research. 2013;50(4):523-532.

Syrian Observatory for Human Rights. More than 570 thousand people were killed on the Syrian territory within 8 years of revolution demanding freedom, democracy, justice, and equality. Retr'd 2 Dec 2019, www.syriahr.com.

United Nations Office for the Coordination of Humanitarian Affairs Occupied Palestinian Territory (OCHA oPt) (2019). Data on casualties. Retr'd 2 Dec 2019, www.ochaopt.org

116–117 Terrorism

Incidents

National Consortium for the Study of Terrorism and Responses to Terrorism (START), University of Maryland. Global Terrorism Database (GTD). 2019.

118–121 Refugees

Where refugees come from

United Nations High Commissioner for Refugees (UNHCR). Global trends: Forced displacement in 2018. Table 2. 2019.

Palestinian territories: Communication Division, United Nations Relief and Works Agency for Palestine Refugees in the Near East (UNRWA) Headquarters. UNRWA in figures 2019. Jerusalem. 2019.

Dispersal of major refugee populations • Where refugees go to

United Nations High Commissioner for Refugees (UNHCR) Global trends: Forced displacement in 2018. Table 1. 2019.

Internally displaced people

International displacement monitoring center (iDMC). 2018 internal displacement figures by country. Retr'd 5 Dec 2019, www.internal-displacement.org

Stateless people

United Nations High Commissioner for Refugees (UNHCR) Global trends: Forced displacement in 2018. Table 7, Excel annex. 2019. www.unhcr.org

122–127 Keeping the peace

Peace agreements since 1990

Bell C et al. PA-X Peace Agreements Database and Dataset, Version 2. 2019.

Cost of violence ...and what it could be spent on

de Coninck H et al. Strengthening and implementing the global response. In: Masson-Delmotte, P et al, editors. Global warming of 1.5°C. 2019.

Institute for Economics & Peace (IEP). Global Peace Index 2019: Measuring peace in a complex world. Sydney: IEP; 2019.

International Federation of Red Cross and Red Crescent Societies (IFRC). The cost of doing nothing: The humanitarian price of climate change and how it can be avoided. Geneva: IFRC; 2019.

Ritchie H, Roser M. Natural disasters: Global damage costs from natural disasters. All natural disasters. Retr'd 20 Dec 2019, www.ourworldindata.org

United Nations Conference on Trade and Development (UNCTAD). Promoting investment in the sustainable development goals. Investment Advisory Series A, number 8. Geneva: UNCTAD; 2018.

UN peacekeeping missions

United Nations Peacekeeping. Where we operate. Retr'd 20 Dec 2019, www.peacekeeping.un.org

Peacekeeping missions

Stockholm International Peace Research Institute (SIPRI). SIPRI yearbook 2019: Armaments, disarmament and international security. Oxford: Oxford University Press; 2019.

United Nations Peacekeeping, op cit.

Forces for peace

United Nations Peacekeeping. Peacekeeping operations Fact Sheet. 30 Sept 2019.

Contributing to peace

United Nations Peacekeeping, op cit. Retr'd 9 Dec 2019

128–131 The new front line

Cyber warfare

Center for Strategic & International Studies (CSIS). Significant cyber incidents since 2006. Retr'd Nov 2019, www.csis.org

Sanger DE. The perfect weapon. War, sabotage, and fear in the cyber age. New York: Crown Publishing Group; 2018.

Kaplan F. Dark territory. The secret history of cyber war. New York: Simon & Schuster; 2017.

Associated Press. China victim of 500,000 cyber-attacks in 2010, says security agency. Guardian, 9 Aug 2011. www.theguardian.com

Beaumont P. Stuxnet worm heralds new era of global cyberwar. Guardian, 30 Sept 2010. www.theguardian.com

Saul J. Global shipping feels fallout from Maersk cyberattack. Reuters, 29 June 2017. www.reuters.com.

Weatherford M. Lessons to be learned from a $10 billion cyberattack. Retr'd from www.whitehawk.com

3D printing

Daase C et al. WMD capabilities enabled by additive manufacturing.

NDS Report 1908. Monterey, CA: Jupiter; 2019.

Bauer S, Brockmann K. 3D printing and missile technology controls. SIPRI Background Paper. Stockholm: Stockholm International Peace Research Institute; Nov 2017. www.sipri.org

Brockmann K. 3D-printable guns and why export controls on technical data matter. SIPRI Commentary/WritePeace blog, 1 Aug 2018. www.sipri.org

Brockmann K. Advances in 3D printing technology: Increasing biological weapon proliferation risks? SIPRI Commentary/WritePeace blog, 29 July 2019. www.sipri.org

Petch M. W3D Printing Community Responds to Covid-19 and Coronavirus Resources. 3D Printing Industry. Retr'd 9 April 2020, from www.3dprintingindustry.com

Artificial intelligence and the arms race

Peldán Carlsson M. Autonomous weapon systems and the impact on strategic stability. Presentation at Rio Seminar on Autonomous Weapon Systems. Rio de Janeiro, Naval War College. 20 Feb 2020. www.funag.gov.br

THE HEALTH OF THE PEOPLE

134–135 Pandemics

Neuman S. Global lockdowns resulting in "horrifying surge" in domestic violence, UN warns. NPR 6 April 2020. www.npr.org

Graham-Harrison E, Giuffrida A, Smith H, Ford L. Lockdowns around the world bring rise in domestic violence. 28 Mar 2020. www.theguardian.com

US Department of Health & Human Services, Centers for Disease Control and Prevention, National Center for Emerging and Zoonotic Infectious Diseases (NCEZID) (2017). "Zoonotic Diseases". Retr'd 4 June 2020, from www.cdc.gov.

The age of epidemics and pandemics

WHO. Summary table of SARS cases by country, 1 November 2002–7 August 2003. www.who.int

WHO. WHO MERS global summary and assessment of risk. August 2018. www.who.int

WHO Regional Office for the Eastern Mediterranean: Monthly MERS Situation updates July 2019 – January 2020. www.wmro.who.int

WHO. Ebola data and statistics. Summary data, as of 11 May 2016. www.apps.who.int

WHO Regional Office for Africa. Ebola Virus Disease Democratic Republic of the Congo. External Situation Report94. 26 May 2020. www.apps.who.int

Centers for Disease Control and Prevention, National Center for Immunization and Respiratory Diseases (NCIRD). 2009 H1N1 Pandemic (H1N1pdm09 virus). Retr'd 8 June 2020 from www.cdc.gov

Rogers S. Full list of swine flu cases, country by country. The Guardian, 28 October 2009. www.theguardian.com

Covid-19 • Covid-19 confirmed cases

WHO. WHO Coronavirus Disease (COVID-19) Dashboard. Retr'd 22 June 2020 from covid19.who.int

136–139 Malnutrition

Undernourished people

World Bank. World Development Indicators: Prevalence of undernourishment (% of population). Retr'd 16 Oct 2019, www.data.worldbank.org

Feeding America: Hunger in America. Retr'd 3 Jan 2020, www.feedingamerica.org

The Trussell Trust. End of year stats. Retr'd 3 Jan 2020, www.trusselltrust.org

Dramatic rise in Germans relying on food banks. 19 Sept 2019. www.dw.com

Undernourishment

Micronutrient deficiencies: Vitamin A deficiency. Retr'd 3 Jan 2020, www.who.int/nutrition/topics/vad/en/

Growing hunger

FAO, IFAD, UNICEF, WFP, WHO. The state of food security and nutrition in the world 2019. Safeguarding against economic slowdowns and downturns. Rome: FAO. Table 1. 2019.

Food shortages

FAO. Crop prospects and food situation. Quarterly Global Report no. 3, Rome: FAO. Sept 2019.

140–143 Obesity

Overweight adults

WHO. Global Health Observatory data repository: Prevalence of overweight among adults. Estimates by country. Retr'd 25 Oct 2019, www.apps.who.int

Impact of obesity

WHO. Obesity and overweight. Key facts. Retr'd 8 Jan 2020, www.who.int

Overweight as cause of death

Institute for Health Metrics and Evaluation (IHME). GBD compare data visualization. Retr'd 30 Oct 2019, www.vizhub.healthdata.org

America's growing obesity problem

Centres for Disease Control and Prevention (CDC). Adult obesity prevalence maps. Retr'd 6 Jan 2020, www.cdc.gov/obesity/data/prevalence-maps.html

144–147 Smoking

Tobacco smokers

WHO. WHO global report on trends in prevalence of tobacco smoking 2000–2025, Table A1.5. Geneva: Author; 2018.

Cigarettes smoked • Smoke-free legislation

American Lung Association. Smokefree air laws. Retr'd 6 Jan 2020, www.lung.org

Drope J et al. The tobacco atlas. Retr'd 30 Oct 2019, www.tobaccoatlas.org

Tobacco-related deaths

Shafey, O, Eriksen M, Ross H, Mackay J. The tobacco atlas, 3rd ed. Atlanta, GA: American Cancer Society; 2009.

148–151 Cancer

World Cancer Research Fund. American Institute for Cancer Research. Comparing more and less developed countries. Retr'd 6 Jan 2020, www.wcrf.org/dietandcancer/cancer-trends/comparing-more-and-less-developed-countries

WHO. Cancer. Key facts. Retr'd 6 Jan 2020, www.who.int

Cancer on the increase

International Agency for Research on Cancer (IARC). World cancer report 2014. Stewart BW, Wild CP, editors. Lyon: Author; 2014.

IARC. World Cancer Report 2008. Boyle P, Levin B, editors. Lyon: Author; 2008.

Jemal A, Torre L, Soerjomataram I, Bray F (eds). The cancer atlas. 3rd ed. Atlanta, GA: American Cancer Society; 2019. www.cancer.org/canceratlas

Childhood-cancer survival rates

Jemal A, op cit.

Environmental factors

Anand P et al. Cancer is a preventable disease that requires major lifestyle changes. Pharmaceutical Research. 2008;25(9):2097–2116.

Cancer in men • Cancer in women

IARC. GLOBOCAN 2018: Top cancer per country, estimated age-standardized incidence rates (World) in 2018, females/males, all ages. Retr'd 28 Oct 2019, www.gco.iarc.fr

152–155 HIV/AIDS

Impact of HIV/AIDS

HIV/AIDS over time

UNAIDS. HIV estimates with uncertainty bounds 1990–2018. 2019. Retr'd 18 Dec 2019, www.unaids.org

AIDS orphans

The World Bank. Health nutrition and population statistics. Retr'd 18 Dec 2019, www.databank.worldbank.org

Barring the door

UNAIDS 2019. AIDSinfo: Epidemic transition metrics – Laws and policies scorecard. Retr'd 4 Nov 2019, www.aidsinfo.unaids.org

Anti-Retroviral Therapy (ART)

UNAIDS. HIV treatment data and estimates 2010-2018.

Text

WHO. Global Health Observatory (GHO) data. HIV/AIDS. Retr'd 7 Jan 2020.

UNAIDS. HIV infections among children falling. 13 May 2019.

156–159 Mental health

Ritchie H, Roser M. Mental Health. Our world in data. Apr 2018. ourworldindata.org/mental-health

WHO. Fact sheet. Adolescent mental health. 23 Oct 2019.

WHO. Fact sheet. Suicide. 2 Sept 2019.

Mental health disorders

Ritchie, op cit.

Spending on mental health • Psychiatrists

WHO. Mental health atlas 2017. Geneva: WHO; 2018.

Suicide by men • Suicide by women

WHO. Global Health Observatory (GHO) data: Age-standardized suicide rates (per 100 000 population), 2016. www.who.int. Retr'd 29 Oct 2019.

160–163 Water and sanitation

WHO, UNICEF. Millennium Development Goal drinking water target met. 6 Mar 2012. www.who.int

WHO, UNICEF. Progress on drinking water, sanitation and hygiene, 2017 update and SDG baselines. 2017.

Drinking water

UNICEF. UNICEF data: Cross-sector indicators. Proportion of population using improved drinking water sources. Retr'd 20 Dec 2019, www.data.unicef.org

Women and girls...

WHO, UNICEF; 2017 op cit.

Sanitation

In 24 countries...

WHO, UNICEF. Estimates on the use of sanitation (2000–17). Joint Monitoring Programme for Sanitation. 2019. www.data.unicef.org

Unsafe schools

WHO, UNICEF. Drinking water, sanitation and hygiene in schools: Global baseline report. 2018. www.data.unicef.org

164–165 Living with disease

WHO. Global Health Observatory (GHO) data. Disability-adjusted life years (DALYs).

National disease burden

Global Health Estimates 2016: Disease burden by cause, age, sex, by country and by region, 2000–16. Geneva, WHO; 2018.

HEALTH OF THE PLANET

Diaz S, Settele J, Brondizio E et al. Summary for policymakers of the global assessment report on biodiversity and ecosystem services of the Intergovernmental Science-Policy Platform on Biodiversity and Ecosystem Services. IPBES: 2019. ipbes.net/global-assessment

168–169 Beyond the bounds

Steffen W et al. Planetary boundaries: Guiding human development on a changing planet. Science 2015;347(6223).

Planetary boundaries

Lokrantz J/Azote based on Steffen et al. 2015 www.stockholmresilience.org/research/planetary-boundaries.html

170–175 Biodiversity Loss

Crowther T, Glick H, Covey K et al.

Mapping tree density at a global scale. Nature 2015;525:201–05.

Khokhar T, Tabary ME. Five forest figures for the International Day of Forests. 21 Mar 2016.

Threatened mammals, birds, and amphibians
IUCN. Table 5: Threatened species in each country (totals by taxonomic group). 2019.

Threatened species
IUCN. Table1a: Number of species evaluated in relation to the overall number of described species, and numbers of threatened species by major groups of organisms. 2019.

Forest lost and gained
FAO. Global forest resources assessment 2015. Desk reference. Second edition. Author: 2015.

Protected areas
World Database on Protected Areas. World Development Indicators: Terrestrial protected areas (% of total land area). The World Bank: 2019. Retr'd 18 Dec 2019, www.data.worldbank.org

Sustainable livelihoods
Rainforest Trust. Conservation in Latin America: Year in review. 27 Dec 2019. www.rainforesttrust.org/conservation-in-latin-america-year-in-review/

Community management
Sunday O. A tale of two Nigerian reserves underscores importance of community. 9 Apr 2020. Mongabay. news.mongabay.com/2020/04/a-tale-of-two-nigerian-reserves-underscores-importance-of-community/

Benefits of forest protection • Preservation and public awareness
12 conservation success stories – in pictures. The Guardian. 22 May 2018. www.theguardian.com

176–179 Water resources
UN. Sustainable Development Goal 6. Synthesis report 2018 on water and sanitation. United Nations: New York; 2018.

Increasing water use
Shiklomanov I. World water resources at the beginning of the 21st century. The dynamics. Table 7. webworld.unesco.org

Burek P et al. Water futures and solutions. Fast track initiative – Final report. ADA Project Number 2725-00/2014). Table 4-10. Laxenburg: IIASA; 2016.

How water is used • Water used • Water stress
FAO. AQUASTAT main database. Retr'd 4 June 2019, www.fao.org

180–183 Waste
McGrath M. US top of the garbage pile in global waste crisis. BBC: 3 July 2019. www.bbc.com/news/science-environment-48838699

World Bank. Trends in solid waste management. datatopics.worldbank.org

Holden E. US produces far more waste and recycles far less of it than other developed countries. Guardian: 3 July 2019.

Cagle S. Humans have made 8.3bn tons of plastic since 1950. Guardian: 24 June 2019. www.theguardian.com

EPA's Report on the Environment (ROE). www.epa.gov/roe

Plastic waste
Belize: Ambergris Today Online (2019). Belize's Single-Use Plastic ban starts today!. Ambergris Today Online. Retr'd 8 Feb 2020, www.ambergistoday.com

Chile: BBC News. Chile bans plastic bags for businesses. BBC News online. 3 Aug 2018. Retr'd 8 Feb 2020, www.bbc.com

China: UNEP, 2018. p.53.

Cyprus: Cyprus introduces plastic bag law. Gold News: 2 July 2018. www.goldnews.com.cy

DR Congo: Soi C. The deadly cost of DR Congo's pollution. Reuters: 2 Oct 2018. www.Aljazeera.com

East African Legislative Assembly: Karuhanga, 2017.

England: Woodcock A. Plastic bag usage in supermarkets down 90 per cent since introduction of 5p charge in 2015. 31 July 2019. www.independent.co.uk

EU and Hong Kong: Single-use plastics. A roadmap for sustainability. Nairobi (Kenya): UNEP: 2018.

France: France to phase out single-use plastics starting Jan 1. France 24: 31 Dec 2019. www.france24.com

Jamaica: Ministry of Economic Growth and Job Creation Jamaica. Statement: Reduction of plastic waste. 2019. www.megjc.gov.jm

Lithuania: Supermarkets in Lithuania to face fines for free plastic bags. Lithuanian Radio and Television: 28 Jan 2020. www.lrt.lt.

New Zealand: Ministry for the Environment, New Zealand. Single-use plastic shopping bags are banned in New Zealand. 2019. www.mfe.govt.nz.

Nigeria: Reps adopt bill banning use of plastic bags, prescribe N500,000 fine. Channels Television. 21 May 2019. www.channelstv.com

Slovenia: No more free plastic bags in Slovenian stores. The Slovenia Times. 2 Jan 2019. www.sloveniatimes.com

Tanzania: Tanzania bans plastic bags to clean up environment. Deutsche Welle: 1 June 2019. www.dw.com

UNEP. Single-use plastics. A roadmap for sustainability. Nairobi (Kenya): UNEP; 2018.

Uruguay: Plastic bags banned in Uruguay, but no hope for larger waste bill. Bloomberg Environment: 29 Jan 2019. www.new.bloombergenvironment.com

What is the great pacific garbage patch? Retr'd 29 Dec 2019, www.theoceancleanup.com

Waste production
World Bank. Global waste to grow by 70 percent by 2050 unless urgent action is taken. Press release: 20 Sept 2018. worldbank.org

Plastic world
PlasticsEurope (2013). Plastics - the Facts 2013, 2015, 2017, 2019. All Retr'd 29 Dec 2019, www.plasticseurope.org

Beach trash
Ocean Conservancy. Annual reports, 2011–2019. oceanconservancy.org

184–185 Oceans

Marine protection
The World Bank. World Development Indicators: Marine protected areas (% of territorial waters). Retr'd 29 Dec 2019, www.data.worldbank.org

Coral reefs
Heron et al. Impacts of climate change on world heritage coral reefs : A first global scientific assessment. Paris: UNESCO World Heritage Centre, 1-2. 2017.

International Union for Conservation of Nature (IUCN) Issue brief: Coral reefs and climate change. 2017. www.iucn.org

Spalding, MD, Brumbaugh RD, Landis E. Atlas of ocean wealth. Arlington, VA: The Nature Conservancy; 2016.

Three examples of reefs: Wikipedia. List of reefs. Retr'd 8 Feb 2020, www.en.wikipedia.org

Seagrass

WWF and ZSL; 2015. op cit.

Mangroves

Bindoff et al. Changing ocean, marine ecosystems, and dependent communities In: IPCC special report on the ocean and cryosphere in a changing climate. 2019. p. 495.

Baxter JM, Laffoley D (eds) Explaining ocean warming. Causes, scale, effects and consequences. Gland: IUCN; 2016. pp. 136-138.

North Atlantic right whales • Blue whales • Whale sharks

WWF. Fact sheets on species. Retr'd 4 Feb 2020, www.worldwildlife.org

Sharks, rays

WWF and ZSL; 2015. op cit.

Neslen A. 40% of Europe's sharks and rays face extinction, says IUCN. The Guardian. 3 June 2015. www.theguardian.com

Ocean dead zones

Carrington D. Oceans suffocating as huge dead zones quadruple since 1950, scientists warn. The Guardian. 4 January 2018. www.theguardian.com

Sea cucumbers

de Greef K. Sea cucumbers are being eaten to death. National Geographic. 14 Nov 2018. www.nationalgeographic.com

World Wildlife Fund International (WWF) & Zoological Society of London (ZSL). Living blue planet report. Species, habitats and human well-being. Gland: WWF and London: ZSL; 2015.

Ocean acidification

Borunda A. Ocean acidification, explained. National Geographic. 7 August 2019. www.nationalgeographic.com

8% of oceans...

UNEP-WCMC and IUCN. Marine protected planet, UNEP-WCMC and IUCN. 2019. www.protectedplanet.net

186–187 Energy

Energy use • Change in energy use

World Bank. World Development Indicators 2019. Retr'd 4 Feb 2020, www.data.worldbank.org

188–191 A changing climate

Past emissions and future consequences • Arctic sea ice

Potsdam Institute for Climate Impact Research. Tipping elements – the Achilles heels of the earth system. Retr'd 25 Jan 2020, www.pik-potsdam.de

Kashiwase H et al. Evidence for ice-ocean albedo feedback in the Arctic Ocean shifting to a seasonal ice zone. Sci Rep. 2017;7:8170. doi. org/10.1038/s41598-017-08467-z

Greenland ice sheet

IPCC. Summary for Policymakers. In: Global Warming of 1.5°C. IPCC; 2018. B.2.2.

West and East Antarctic ice sheets

Potsdam Institute for Climate Impact Research. op cit.

Lenton TM et al. Climate tipping points – too risky to bet against. Nature. 27 Nov 2019. www.nature.com

World's oceans

Potsdam Institute for Climate Impact Research. op cit.

Permafrost

IPCC, op cit. Table 3.7.

Amazon rainforest

Gatehouse G. Deforested parts of Amazon 'emitting more CO2 than they absorb'. BBC News. 11 Feb 2020. www.bbc.com

CO$_2$ in atmosphere

Tans P. NOAA/ESRL (www.esrl.noaa. gov/gmd/ccgg/trends/), Keeling R, Scripps Institution of Oceanography (scrippsco2.ucsd.edu/). Accessed Mar 2020 from: Global Monitoring Laboratory. Mauna Loa CO$_2$ records.

Human cost of natural disasters • Financial cost of natural disasters

Centre for Research on the Epidemiology of Disasters (CRED) (2020). EM-DAT. The International Disaster Database. Data as of 30 Jan 2020. www.emdat.be

Text

United Nations (UN). Paris Agreement. 2015. sustainabledevelopment.un.org

Timetable for changing course • Sectoral changes

Schaeffer M et al. Insights from the IPCC Special Report on 1.5°C for preparation of long-term strategies. Berlin (Germany): Climate Analytics gGmbH; 2019.

IPCC. Summary for Policymakers. In: Global Warming of 1.5°C. IPCC; 2018.

194–197 A greening world

Energy & Climate Intelligence Unit. www.eciu.net

ITV. World sees growing move towards net zero emissions goals – analysis. 18 Feb 2020. www.itv.com

Commitment to net zero emissions

Climate Analytics & New Climate Institute. Climate Action Tracker: Countries. Retr'd 7 Mar 2020, www.climateactiontracker.org

Energy & Climate Intelligence Unit. Net zero tracker. Retr'd 8 Mar 2020, www.eciu.net

Divestment from fossil fuels

350.org. 1000+ divestment commitments. Overview. Retr'd 16 Mar 2020, www.gofossilfree.org

Growth in Renewables

REN21. Renewables Global Status Report. Paris: REN21 Secretariat. 2009–2019.

The Great Green Wall

United Nations Convention to Combat Desertification (2020). Partner countries. Retr'd 16 Mar 2020, www.greatgreenwall.org

Baker A, Toubab M. Can a 4,815-mile wall of trees help curb climate change in Africa? Time. 12 Sept 2019. www.time.com

United Nations Convention to Combat Desertification. The Great Green Wall Initiative. Retr'd 8 Mar 2020, www.unccd.int

Index